ECONOMIC POLICY

Ludwig von Mises

ECONOMIC POLICY
Thoughts for Today and Tomorrow

REGNERY GATEWAY, INC.

Chicago

Published by Regnery Gateway, Inc. Book Publishers
360 West Superior Street, Chicago, Illinois 60610
Manufactured in the United States of America.

Library of Congress Catalog Card Number: 79-65851
International Standard Book Number: 0-89526-899-X

Contents

Foreword

The present book fully reflects the
author's fundamental position for which
he was—and still is—admired by followers
and reviled by opponents. . . . While each of
the six lectures can stand alone as an
independent essay, the harmony of the
series gives an aesthetic pleasure similar
to that derived from looking at the
architecture of a well-designed edifice.
—Fritz Machlup
Princeton, 1979

Late in 1958, when my husband was invited by Dr. Alberto Benegas-Lynch to come to Argentina and deliver a series of lectures, I was asked to accompany him. This book contains, in written word, what my husband said to hundreds of Argentinian students in those lectures.

We arrived in Argentina some months after Peron had been forced to leave the country. He had governed destructively and completely destroyed Argentina's economic foundations. His successor, Eduardo Lonardi, was not much better. The nation was ready for new ideas, and my husband was equally ready to provide them.

His lectures were delivered in English, in the enormous lecture hall of the University of Buenos Aires. In two neighboring rooms his words were simultaneously

vii

translated into Spanish for students who listened with earphones. Ludwig von Mises spoke without any restraint about capitalism, socialism, interventionism, communism, fascism, economic policy and the dangers of dictatorship. These young people, who listened to my husband, did not know much about freedom of the market or individual freedom. As I wrote about this occasion in *My Years with Ludwig von Mises*, "If anyone in those times would have dared to attack communism and fascism as my husband did, the police would have come in and taken hold of him immediately, and the assembly would have been broken up."

The audience reacted as if a window had been opened and fresh air allowed to breeze through the rooms. He spoke without any notes. As always, his thoughts were guided by just a few words, written on a scrap of paper. He knew exactly what he wanted to say, and by using comparatively simple terms, he succeeded in communicating his ideas to an audience not familiar with his work, so that they could understand exactly what he was saying.

The lectures were taped, and the tapes were later transcribed by a Spanish-speaking secretary whose typed manuscript I found among my husband's posthumous papers. On reading the transcript, I remembered vividly the singular enthusiasm with which those Argentinians had responded to my husband's words. And it seemed to me, as a non-economist, that these lectures, delivered to a lay audience in South America, were much easier to understand than many of Ludwig von Mises' more theoretical writings. I felt they contained so much valuable material, so many thoughts important for today and the future, that they should be made available to the public.

Since my husband had never revised the transcripts of his lectures for book publication, that task remained for me. I have been very careful to keep intact the meaning of every sentence, to change nothing of the content and to preserve all the expressions my husband often used which are so familiar to his readers. My only contribution has been to pull the sentences together and take out some of the little words one uses when talking informally. If my attempt to convert these lectures into a book has succeeded, it is only due to the fact that, with every sentence, I heard my husband's voice, I heard him talk. He was alive to me, alive in how clearly he demonstrated the evil and danger of too much government; how comprehensibly and lucidly he described the differences between dictatorship and interventionism; with how much wit he talked about important historic personalities; with how few remarks he succeeded in making bygone times come alive.

I want to use this opportunity to thank my good friend George Koether for assisting me with this task. His editorial experience and his understanding of my husband's theories were a great help to this book.

I hope these lectures will be read not only by scholars but also by my husband's many admirers among non-economists. And I earnestly hope that this book will be made available to younger audiences, especially high school and college students around the world.

MARGIT VON MISES
New York
June 1979

Capitalism

Descriptive terms which people use are often quite misleading. In talking about modern captains of industry and leaders of big business, for instance, they call a man a "chocolate king" or a "cotton king" or an "automobile king." Their use of such terminology implies that they see practically no difference between the modern heads of industry and those feudal kings, dukes or lords of earlier days. But the difference is in fact very great, for a chocolate king does not rule at all, he *serves*. He does not reign over conquered territory, independent of the market, independent of his customers. The chocolate king—or the steel king or the automobile king or any other king of modern industry—depends on the industry he operates and on the customers he serves. This "king" must stay in the good graces of his subjects, the consumers; he loses his "kingdom" as soon as he is no longer in a position to give his customers better service and provide it at lower cost than others with whom he must compete.

Two hundred years ago, before the advent of capitalism, a man's social status was fixed from the beginning to the end of his life; he inherited it from his ancestors, and it never changed. If he was born poor, he always remained poor, and if he was born rich—a lord or a duke—he kept his dukedom and the property that went with it for the rest of his life.

As for manufacturing, the primitive processing industries of those days existed almost exclusively for the benefit of the wealthy. Most of the people (ninety percent or more of the European population) worked the land and did not come in contact with the city-oriented processing industries. This rigid system of feudal society prevailed in the most developed areas of Europe for many hundreds of years.

However, as the rural population expanded, there developed a surplus of people on the land. For this surplus of population without inherited land or estates, there was not enough to do, nor was it possible for them to work in the processing industries; the kings of the cities denied them access. The numbers of these "outcasts" continued to grow, and still no one knew what to do with them. They were, in the full sense of the word, "proletarians," outcasts whom the government could only put into the workhouse or the poorhouse. In some sections of Europe, especially in the Netherlands and in England, they became so numerous that, by the eighteenth century, they were a real menace to the preservation of the prevailing social system.

Today, in discussing similar conditions in places like India or other developing countries, we must not forget that, in eighteenth-century England, conditions were much worse. At that time, England had a population of six or seven million people, but of those six or seven million people, more than one million, probably two million, were simply poor outcasts for whom the existing social system made no provision. What to do with these outcasts was one of the great problems of eighteenth-century England.

Another great problem was the lack of raw materials. The British, very seriously, had to ask themselves this question: what are we going to do in the future, when our forests will no longer give us the wood we need for our industries and for heating our houses? For the ruling classes it was a desperate situation. The statesmen did not know what to do, and the ruling gentry were absolutely without any ideas on how to improve conditions.

Out of this serious social situation emerged the beginnings of modern capitalism. There were some persons among those outcasts, among those poor people, who tried to organize others to set up small shops which could produce something. This was an innovation. These innovators did not produce expensive goods suitable only for the upper classes; they produced cheaper products for everyone's needs. And this was the origin of capitalism as it operates today. It was *the beginning of mass production*, the fundamental principle of capitalistic industry. Whereas the old processing industries serving the rich people in the cities had existed almost exclusively for the demands of the upper classes, the new capitalist industries began to produce things that could be purchased by the general population. It was mass production to satisfy the needs of the masses.

This is the fundamental principle of capitalism as it exists today in all of those countries in which there is a highly developed system of mass production: Big business, the target of the most fanatic attacks by the so-called leftists, produces almost exclusively to satisfy the wants of the masses. Enterprises producing luxury goods solely for the well-to-do can never attain the magnitude of big businesses. And today, it is the people who work in large factories who are the main consumers of the products made in those factories. This is the fundamental difference between the capitalistic principles of production and the feudalistic principles of the preceding ages.

When people assume, or claim, that there is a difference between the producers and the consumers of the products of big businesses, they are badly mistaken. In American department stores you hear the slogan, "the customer is always right." And this customer is the same man who produces in the factory those things which are sold in the department stores. The people who think that the power of big business is enormous are mistaken also, since big business depends entirely on the patronage of those who buy its products: the biggest enterprise loses its power and its influence when it loses its customers.

Fifty or sixty years ago it was said in almost all capitalist countries that the railroad companies were too big and too powerful; they had a monopoly; it was impossible to compete with them. It was alleged that, in the field of transportation, capitalism had already reached a stage at which it had destroyed itself, for it had eliminated competition. What people overlooked was the fact that the power of the railroads depended on their ability to serve people better than any other method of transportation. Of course it would have been ridiculous to compete with one of these big railroad companies by building another railroad parallel to the old line, since the old line was sufficient to serve existing needs. But very soon there came other competitors. Freedom of competition does not mean that you can succeed simply by imitating or copying precisely what someone else has done. Freedom of the press does not mean that you have the right to copy what another man has written and thus to acquire the success which this other man has duly merited on account of his achievements. It means that you have the right to write something different. Freedom of competition concerning railroads, for example, means that you are free to invent something, to do something, which will challenge the railroads and place them in a very precarious competitive situation.

In the United States the competition to the railroads—in the form of buses, automobiles, trucks, and airplanes—has caused the railroads to suffer and to be almost completely defeated, as far as passenger transportation is concerned.

The development of capitalism consists in everyone's having the right to serve the customer better and/or more cheaply. And this method, this principle, has, within a comparatively short time, transformed the whole world. It has made possible an unprecedented increase in world population.

In eighteenth-century England, the land could support only six million people at a very low standard of living. Today more than fifty million people enjoy a much higher standard of living than even the rich enjoyed during the eighteenth-century. And today's standard of living in England would probably be still higher, had not a great deal of the energy of the British been wasted in what were, from various points of view, avoidable political and military "adventures."

These are the facts about capitalism. Thus, if an Englishman—or, for that matter, any other man in any country of the world—says today to his friends that he is opposed to capitalism, there is a wonderful way to answer him: "You know that the population of this planet is now ten times greater than it was in the ages preceding capitalism; you know that all men today enjoy a higher standard of living than your ancestors did before the age of capitalism. But how do you know that you are the one

out of ten who would have lived in the absence of
capitalism? The mere fact that you are living today is
proof that capitalism has succeeded, whether or not you
consider your own life very valuable."

In spite of all its benefits, capitalism has been furiously
attacked and criticized. It is necessary that we understand the origin of this antipathy. It is a fact that the
hatred of capitalism originated *not* with the masses, *not*
among the workers themselves, but among the landed
aristocracy—the gentry of England and the European
continent. They blamed capitalism for something that
was not very pleasant for them: at the beginning of the
nineteenth century, the higher wages paid by industry to
its workers forced the landed gentry to pay equally
higher wages to their *agricultural* workers. The aristocracy attacked the industries by criticising the standard of
living of the masses of the workers.

Of course—from our viewpoint, the workers' standard
of living was extremely low; conditions under early
capitalism were absolutely shocking, but not because the
newly developed capitalistic industries had harmed the
workers. The people hired to work in factories had already been existing at a virtually subhuman level.

The famous old story, repeated hundreds of times,
that the factories employed women and children and
that these women and children, before they were working in factories, had lived under satisfactory conditions,
is one of the greatest falsehoods of history. The mothers
who worked in the factories had nothing to cook with;
they did not leave their homes and their kitchens to go
into the factories, they went into factories because they
had no kitchens, and if they had a kitchen they had no
food to cook in those kitchens. And the children did not
come from comfortable nurseries. They were starving

and dying. And all the talk about the so-called unspeakable horror of early capitalism can be refuted by a single statistic: precisely in these years in which British capitalism developed, precisely in the age called the Industrial Revolution in England, in the years from 1760 to 1830, precisely in those years the population of England doubled, which means that hundreds or thousands of children—who would have died in preceding time—survived and grew to become men and women.

There is no doubt that the conditions of the preceding times were very unsatisfactory. It was capitalist business that improved them. It was precisely those early factories that provided for the needs of their workers, either directly or indirectly by exporting products and importing food and raw materials from other countries. Again and again, the early historians of capitalism have—one can hardly use a milder word—falsified history.

One anecdote they used to tell, quite possibly invented, involved Benjamin Franklin. According to the story, Ben Franklin visited a cotton mill in England, and the owner of the mill told him, full of pride: "Look, here are cotton goods for Hungary." Benjamin Franklin, looking around, seeing that the workers were shabbily dressed, said: "Why don't you produce also for your own workers?"

But those exports of which the owner of the mill spoke really meant that he *did* produce for his own workers, because England had to import all its raw materials. There was no cotton either in England or in continental Europe. There was a shortage of food in England, and food had to be imported from Poland, from Russia, from Hungary. These exports were the payment for the imports of the food which made the survival of the British population possible. Many examples from the history of

those ages will show the attitude of the gentry and aristocracy toward the workers. I want to cite only two
examples. One is the famous British "seed and land"
system. By this system, the British government paid all
workers who did not get the minimum wage (determined by the government) the difference between the
wages they received and this minimum wage. This saved
the landed aristocracy the trouble of paying higher
wages. The gentry would pay the traditionally low agricultural wage, and the government would supplement
it, thus keeping workers from leaving rural occupations
to seek urban factory employment.

Eighty years later, after capitalism's expansion from
England to continental Europe, the landed aristocracy
again reacted against the new production system. In
Germany the Prussian Junkers, having lost many workers to the higher-paying capitalistic industries, invented
a special term for the problem: "flight from the
countryside"—*Landflucht*. And in the German Parliament, they discussed what might be done against this
evil, as it was seen from the point of view of the landed
aristocracy. Prince Bismarck, the famous chancellor of
the German Reich, in a speech one day said, "I met a man
in Berlin who once had worked on my estate, and I asked
this man, 'Why did you leave the estate; why did you go
away from the country; why are you now living in Berlin?' "

And, according to Bismarck, this man answered, "You
don't have such a nice *Biergarten* in the village as we have
here in Berlin, where you can sit, drink beer, and listen to
music." This is, of course, a story told from the point of
view of Prince Bismarck, the employer. It was not the
point of view of all his employees. They went into industry because industry paid them higher wages and raised

their standard of living to an unprecendented degree. Today, in the capitalist countries, there is relatively little difference between the basic life of the so-called higher and lower classes; both have food, clothing, and shelter. But in the eighteenth century and earlier, the difference between the man of the middle class and the man of the lower class was that the man of the middle class had shoes and the man of the lower class did *not* have shoes. In the United States today the difference between a rich man and a poor man means very often only the difference between a Cadillac and a Chevrolet. The Chevrolet may be bought secondhand, but basically it renders the same services to its owner: he, too, can drive from one point to another. More than fifty percent of the people in the United States are living in houses and apartments they own themselves.

The attacks against capitalism—especially with respect to the higher wage rates—start from the false assumption that wages are ultimately paid by people who are different from those who are employed in the factories. Now it is all right for economists and for students of economic theories to distinguish between the worker and the consumer and to make a distinction between them. But the fact is that every consumer must, in some way or the other, earn the money he spends, and the immense majority of the consumers are precisely the same people who work as employees in the enterprises that produce the things which they consume. Wage rates under capitalism are not set by a class of people different from the class of people who earn the wages: they are the *same* people. It is *not* the Hollywood film corporation that pays the wages of a movie star; it is the people who pay admission to the movies. And it is *not* the entrepreneur of a boxing match who pays the enormous demands of the prize fighters; it is the people who pay admission to the fight. Through the distinction between the employer and the employee, a distinction is drawn in economic theory, but it is not a distinction in real life; here, the employer and the employee ultimately are one and the same person.

There are people in many countries who consider it very unjust that a man who has to support a family with several children will receive the same salary as a man who has only himself to take care of. But the question is not whether the employer should bear greater responsibility for the size of a worker's family.

The question we must ask in this case is: Are you, as an individual, prepared to pay *more* for something, let us say, a loaf of bread, if you are told that the man who produced this loaf of bread has six children? The honest man will certainly answer in the negative and say, "In principle I would, but in fact I would rather buy the bread produced by a man without any children." The fact is that, if the buyers do not pay the employer enough to enable him to pay his workers, it becomes impossible for the employer to remain in business.

The capitalist system was termed "capitalism" not by a friend of the system, but by an individual who considered it to be the worst of all historical systems, the greatest evil that had ever befallen mankind. That man was Karl Marx. Nevertheless, there is no reason to reject Marx's term, because it describes clearly the source of the great social improvements brought about by capitalism. Those improvements are the result of capital accumulation; they are based on the fact that people, as a rule, do not consume everything they have produced, that they save—and invest—a part of it. There is a great deal of misunderstanding about this problem and—in the course of these six lectures—I will have the opportunity to deal with the most fundamental misapprehensions which people have concerning the accumulation of capital, the use of capital, and the universal advantages to be gained from such use. I will deal with capitalism particularly in my lectures about foreign investment and about that most critical problem of present-day politics, inflation. You know, of course, that inflation exists not only in this country. It is a problem all over the world today.

An often unrealized fact about capitalism is this: savings mean benefits for all those who are anxious to produce or to earn wages. When a man has accrued a certain amount of money—let us say, one thousand dollars—and, instead of spending it, entrusts these dollars to a savings bank or an insurance company, the money goes into the hands of an entrepreneur, a businessman, enabling him to go out and embark on a project which could not have been embarked on yesterday, because the required capital was unavailable.

What will the businessman do now with the additional capital? The first thing he must do, the first use he will make of this additional capital, is to go out and hire workers and buy raw materials—in turn causing a *further* demand for workers and raw materials to develop, as well as a tendency toward higher wages and higher prices for raw materials. Long before the saver or the entrepreneur obtain any profit from all of this, the unemployed worker, the producer of raw materials, the farmer, and the wage-earner are all sharing in the benefits of the additional savings.

Whether the entrepreneur will get something out of the project depends on the future state of the market and on his ability to anticipate correctly the future state of the market. But the workers as well as the producers of raw materials get the benefits immediately. Much was said, thirty or forty years ago, about the "wage policy," as they called it, of Henry Ford. One of Mr. Ford's great accomplishments was that he paid higher wages than did other industrialists or factories. His wage policy was described as an "invention," yet it is not enough to say that this new "invented" policy was the result of the liberality of Mr. Ford. A new branch of business, or a new factory in an already existing branch of business, has to attract workers from *other* employments, from other parts of the country, even from other countries. And the only way to do this is to offer the workers higher wages for their work. This is what took place in the early days of capitalism, and it is still taking place today.

When the manufacturers in Great Britain first began to produce cotton goods, they paid their workers more than they had earned before. Of course, a great percentage of these new workers had earned nothing at all before that and were prepared to take anything they were offered. But after a short time—when more and more capital was accumulated and more and more new enterprises were developed—wage rates went up, and the result was the unprecedented increase in British population which I spoke of earlier.

The scornful depiction of capitalism by some people as a system designed to make the rich become richer and the poor become poorer is wrong from beginning to end. Marx's thesis regarding the coming of socialism was based on the assumption that workers *were* getting poorer, that the masses *were* becoming more destitute, and that finally all the wealth of a country would be concentrated in a few hands or in the hands of one man only. And then the masses of impoverished workers would finally rebel and expropriate the riches of the wealthy proprietors. According to this doctrine of Karl Marx, there can be no opportunity, no possibility within the capitalistic system for any improvement of the conditions of the workers.

In 1865, speaking before the International Workingmen's Association in England, Marx said the belief that labor unions could improve conditions for the working population was "absolutely in error." The union policy of asking for higher wage rates and shorter work hours he called *conservative*—conservatism being, of course, the most condemnatory term which Karl Marx could use. He suggested that the unions set themselves a new, *revolutionary* goal: that they "do away with the wage system altogether," that they substitute "socialism"—government ownership of the means of production—for the system of private ownership.

If we look upon the history of the world, and especially upon the history of England since 1865, we realize that Marx was wrong in every respect. There is no western, capitalistic country in which the conditions of the masses have not improved in an unprecedented way. All these improvements of the last eighty or ninety years were made *in spite of* the prognostications of Karl Marx. For the Marxian socialists believed that the conditions of the workers could never be ameliorated. They followed a false theory, the famous "iron law of wages"—the law which stated that a worker's wages, under capitalism, would not exceed the amount he needed to sustain his life for service to the enterprise.

The Marxians formulated their theory in this way: if the workers' wage rates go up, raising wages above the subsistence level, they will have more children; and these children, when they enter the labor force, will increase the number of workers to the point where the wage rates will drop, bringing the workers once more down to the subsistence level—to that minimal sustenance level which will just barely prevent the working population from dying out.

But this idea of Marx, and of many other socialists, is a concept of the working man precisely like that which biologists use—and rightly so—in studying the life of animals. Of mice, for instance.

If you increase the quantity of food available for animal organisms or for microbes, then more of them will survive. And if you restrict their food, then you will restrict their numbers. But man is different. Even the worker—in spite of the fact that Marxists do not acknowledge it—has human wants other than food and reproduction of his species. An increase in real wages results not only in an increase in population, it results also, and first of all, in an *improvement in the average standard of living*. That is why today we have a higher standard of living in Western Europe and in the United States than in the developing nations of, say, Africa.

We must realize, however, that this higher standard of living depends on the supply of capital. This explains the difference between conditions in the United States and conditions in India; modern methods of fighting contagious diseases have been introduced in India—at least, to some extent—and the effect has been an unprecedented increase in population but, since this increase in population has not been accompanied by a corresponding increase in the amount of capital invested, the result has been an increase in poverty. *A country becomes more prosperous in proportion to the rise in the invested capital per unit of its population.*

I hope that in my other lectures I will have the opportunity to deal in greater detail with these problems and will be able to clarify them, because some terms—such as "the capital invested per capita"—require a rather detailed explanation.

But you have to remember that, in economic policies, there are no miracles. You have read in many newspapers and speeches, about the so-called German economic miracle—the recovery of Germany after its defeat and destruction in the Second World War. But this was no miracle. It was the application of the *principles of the free market economy*, of the methods of capitalism, even though they were not applied completely in all respects. Every country can experience the same "miracle" of economic recovery, although I must insist that economic recovery does *not* come from a miracle; it comes from the adoption of—and is the result of—sound economic policies.

2nd Lecture

Socialism

I am here in Buenos Aires as a guest of the Institute por la Economía Libre. What is *economía libre?* What does this system of economic freedom mean? The answer is simple: it is the market economy, it is the system in which the cooperation of individuals in the social division of labor is achieved by the market. This market is not a place; it is a *process*, it is the way in which, by selling and buying, by producing and consuming, the individuals contribute to the total workings of society.

In dealing with this system of economic organization—the market economy—we employ the term "economic freedom." Very often, people misunderstand what it means, believing that economic freedom is something quite apart from other freedoms, and that these other freedoms—which they hold to be more important—can be preserved even in the absence of economic freedom. The meaning of economic freedom is this: that the individual is in a position to *choose* the way in which he wants to integrate himself into the totality of society. The individual is able to choose his career, he is free to do what he *wants* to do.

This is of course not meant in the sense which so many people attach to the word freedom today; it is meant rather in the sense that, through economic freedom, man is freed from natural conditions. In nature, there is nothing that can be termed freedom, there is only the regularity of the laws of nature, which man must obey if he wants to attain something.

In using the term freedom as applied to human beings, we think only of the freedom *within society*. Yet, today, social freedoms are considered by many people to be independent of each another. Those who call themselves "liberals" today are asking for policies which are precisely the opposite of those policies which the liberals of the nineteenth century advocated in their liberal programs. The so-called liberals of today have the very popular idea that freedom of speech, of thought, of the press, freedom of religion, freedom from imprisonment without trial—that all these freedoms can be preserved in the absence of what is called economic freedom. They do not realize that, in a system where there is no market, where the government directs everything, all those other freedoms are illusory, even if they are made into laws and written up in constitutions.

Let us take one freedom, the freedom of the press. If the government owns all the printing presses, it will determine what is to be printed and what is not to be printed. And if the government owns all the printing presses and determines what shall or shall not be printed, then the possibility of printing any kind of opposing arguments against the ideas of the government becomes practically nonexistent. Freedom of the press disappears. And it is the same with all the other freedoms.

In a market economy, the individual has the freedom to choose whatever career he wishes to pursue, to choose his own way of integrating himself into society. But in a socialist system, that is not so: his career is decided by decree of the government. The government can order people whom it dislikes, whom it does not want to live in certain regions, to move into other regions and to other places. And the government is always in a position to justify and to explain such procedure by declaring that the governmental plan requires the presence of this eminent citizen five thousand miles away from the place in which he could be disagreeable to those in power.

It is true that the freedom a man may have in a market economy is not a perfect freedom from the metaphysical point of view. But there is no such thing as perfect freedom. Freedom means something only within the framework of society. The eighteenth-century authors of "natural law"—above all, Jean Jacques Rousseau— believed that once, in the remote past, men enjoyed something called "natural" freedom. But in that remote age, individuals were not free, they were at the mercy of everyone who was stronger than they were. The famous words of Rousseau: "Man is born free and everywhere he is in chains" may sound good, but man is in fact *not* born free. Man is born a very weak suckling. Without the protection of his parents, without the protection given to his parents by society, he would not be able to preserve his life.

Freedom in society means that a man depends as much upon other people as other people depend upon him. Society under the market economy, under the conditions of "economía libre," means a state of affairs in which everybody serves his fellow citizens and is served by them in return. People believe that there are in the market economy bosses who are independent of the good will and support of other people. They believe that the captains of industry, the businessmen, the entrepreneurs are the real bosses in the economic system. But this is an illusion. The real bosses in the economic system are the consumers. And if the consumers stop patronizing a branch of business, these businessmen are either forced to abandon their eminent position in the economic system or to adjust their actions to the wishes and to the orders of the consumers.

One of the best-known propagators of communism was Lady Passfield, under her maiden name Beatrice Potter, and well-known under the name of her husband Sydney Webb. This lady was the daughter of a wealthy businessman and, when she was a young adult, she served as her father's secretary. In her memoirs she writes: "In the business of my father everybody had to obey the orders issued by my father, the boss. He alone had to give orders, but to him nobody gave any orders." This is a very short-sighted view. Orders *were* given to her father by the consumers, by the buyers. Unfortunately, she could not see *these* orders; she could not see what goes on in a market economy, because she was interested only in the orders given within her father's office or his factory.

In all economic problems, we must bear in mind the words of the great French economist Frédéric Bastiat, who titled one of his brilliant essays: *"Ce qu'on voit et ce qu'on ne voit pas"* ("What you see and what you do not see"). In order to comprehend the operation of an economic system, we must deal not only with the things that can be seen, but we also have to give our attention to the things which cannot be perceived directly. For instance, an order issued by a boss to an office boy can be heard by everybody who is present in the room. What cannot be heard are the orders given to the boss by his customers.

The fact is that, under the capitalistic system, the ultimate bosses are the consumers. The sovereign is not the state, it is the people. And the proof that they are the sovereign is borne out by the fact that they have *the right to be foolish*. This is the privilege of the sovereign. He has the right to make mistakes, no one can prevent him from making them, but of course he has to pay for his mistakes. If we say the consumer is supreme or that the consumer is sovereign, we do not say that the consumer is free from faults, that the consumer is a man who always knows what would be best for him. The consumers very often buy things or consume things they ought not to buy or ought not to consume.

But the notion that a capitalist form of government can prevent people from hurting themselves by controlling their consumption is false. The idea of government as a paternal authority, as a guardian for everybody, is the idea of those who favor socialism. In the United States some years ago, the government tried what was called "a noble experiment." This noble experiment was a law making it illegal to consume intoxicating beverages. It is certainly true that many people drink too much brandy and whiskey, and that they may hurt themselves by doing so. Some authorities in the United States are even opposed to smoking. Certainly there are many people who smoke too much and who smoke in spite of the fact that it would be better for them not to smoke. This raises a question which goes far beyond economic discussion: it shows what freedom really means.

Granted, that it is good to keep people from hurting themselves by drinking or smoking too much. But once you have admitted this, other people will say: Is the body everything? Is not the mind of man much more important? Is not the mind of man the real human endowment, the real human quality? If you give the government the right to determine the consumption of the human body, to determine whether one should smoke or not smoke, drink or not drink, there is no good reply you can give to people who say: "More important than the body is the mind and the soul, and man hurts himself much more by reading bad books, by listening to bad music and looking at bad movies. Therefore it is the duty of the government to prevent people from committing these faults."

And, as you know, for many hundreds of years governments and authorities believed that this really *was* their duty. Nor did this happen in far distant ages only; not long ago, there was a government in Germany that considered it a governmental duty to distinguish between good and bad paintings—which of course meant good and bad from the point of view of a man who, in his youth, had failed the entrance examination at the Academy of Art in Vienna; good and bad from the point of view of a picture-postcard painter. And it became illegal for people to utter other views about art and paintings than those of the Supreme Führer.

Once you begin to admit that it is the duty of the government to control your consumption of alcohol, what can you reply to those who say the control of books and ideas is much more important?

Freedom really means *the freedom to make mistakes*. This we have to realize. We may be highly critical with regard to the way in which our fellow citizens are spending their money and living their lives. We may believe that what they are doing is absolutely foolish and bad, but in a free society, there are many ways for people to air their opinions on how their fellow citizens should change their ways of life. They can write books; they can write articles; they can make speeches; they can even preach at street corners if they want—and they do this, in many countries. But they must *not* try to police other people in order to prevent them from doing certain things simply because they themselves do not want these other people to have the freedom to do it.

This is the difference between slavery and freedom. The slave must do what his superior orders him to do, but the free citizen—and this is what freedom means—is in a position to choose his own way of life. Certainly this capitalistic system can be abused, and is abused, by some people. It is certainly possible to do things which ought not to be done. But if these things are approved by a majority of the people, a disapproving person always has a way to attempt to change the minds of his fellow citizens. He can try to persuade them, to convince them, but he may not try to force them by the use of power, of governmental police power.

In the market economy, everyone serves his fellow citizens by serving himself. This is what the liberal authors of the eighteenth century had in mind when they spoke of the harmony of the rightly understood interests of all groups and of all individuals of the population. And it was this doctrine of the harmony of interests which the socialists opposed. They spoke of an "irreconcilable conflict of interests" between various groups.

What does this mean? When Karl Marx—in the first chapter of the *Communist Manifesto*, that small pamphlet which inaugurated his socialist movement—claimed that there was an irreconcilable conflict between classes, he could not illustrate his thesis by any examples other than those drawn from the conditions of precapitalistic society. In precapitalistic ages, society was divided into hereditary status groups, which in India are called "castes." In a status society a man was not, for example, born a Frenchman; he was born as a member of the French aristocracy or of the French bourgeoisie or of the

French peasantry. In the greater part of the Middle Ages, he was simply a serf. And serfdom, in France, did not disappear completely until after the American Revolution. In other parts of Europe it disappeared even later.

But the worst form in which serfdom existed—and continued to exist even after the abolition of slavery—was in the British colonies abroad. The individual inherited his status from his parents, and he retained it throughout his life. He transferred it to his children. Every group had privileges and disadvantages. The highest groups had only privileges, the lowest groups only disadvantages. And there was no way a man could rid himself of the legal disadvantages placed upon him by his status other than by fighting a political struggle against the other classes. Under such conditions, you could say that there was an "irreconcilable conflict of interests between the slave owners and the slaves," because what the slaves wanted was to be rid of their slavery, of their quality of being slaves. This meant a loss, however, for the owners. Therefore there is no question that there had to be this irreconcilable conflict of interests between the members of the various classes.

One must not forget that in those ages—in which the status societies were predominant in Europe, as well as in the colonies which the Europeans later founded in America—people did not consider themselves to be connected in any special way with the other classes of their own nation; they felt much more at one with the members of their own class in other countries. A French aristocrat did not look upon lower class Frenchmen as his fellow citizens; they were the "rabble," which he did not like. He regarded only the aristocrats of other countries—those of Italy, England, and Germany—for instance, as his equals.

The most visible effect of this state of affairs was the fact that the aristocrats all over Europe used the same language. And this language was French, a language which was not understood, outside France, by other groups of the population. The middle classes—the bourgeoisie—had their own language, while the lower classes—the peasantry—used local dialects which very often were not understood by other groups of the population. The same was true with regard to the way people dressed. When you travelled in 1750 from one country to another, you found that the upper classes, the aristocrats, were usually dressed in the same way all over Europe, and you found that the lower classes dressed differently. When you met someone in the street, you could see immediately—from the way he dressed—to which class, to which status he belonged.

It is difficult to imagine how different these conditions were from present-day conditions. When I come from the United States to Argentina and I see a man on the street, I cannot know what his status is. I only assume that he is a citizen of Argentina and that he is not a member of some legally restricted group. This is one thing that capitalism has brought about. Of course, there are also differences within capitalism. There are differences in wealth, differences which Marxians mistakenly consider to be equivalent to the old differences that existed between men in the status society.

The differences within a capitalist society are not the same as those in a socialist society. In the Middle Ages—and in many countries even much later—a family could be an aristocrat family and possess great wealth, it could be a family of dukes for hundreds and hundreds of years, whatever its qualities, its talents, its character or morals. But, under modern capitalistic conditions, there is what has been technically described by sociologists as "social mobility." The operating principle of this social mobility, according to the Italian sociologist and economist Vilfredo Pareto, is "la circulation des élites" (the circulation of the elites). This means that there are always people who are at the top of the social ladder, who are wealthy, who are politically important, but these people—these elites—are continually changing.

This is perfectly true in a capitalist society. It was *not* true for a precapitalistic status society. The families who were considered the great aristocratic families of Europe are still the same families today or, let us say, they are the descendants of families that were foremost in Europe, 800 or 1000 or more years ago. The Capetians of Bourbon—who for a very long time ruled here in Argentina—were a royal house as early as the tenth century. These kings ruled the territory which is known now as the Ile-de-France, extending their reign from generation to generation. But in a capitalist society, there is continuous mobility—poor people becoming rich and the descendants of those rich people losing their wealth and becoming poor.

Today I saw in a bookshop in one of the central streets of Buenos Aires the biography of a businessman who was so eminent, so important, so characteristic of big business in the nineteenth century in Europe that, even in this country, far away from Europe, the bookshop carried copies of his biography. I happen to know the grandson of this man. He has the same name his grandfather had, and he still has a right to wear the title of nobility which his grandfather—who started as a blacksmith—had received eighty years ago. Today this grandson is a poor photographer in New York City.

Other people, who were poor at the time this photographer's grandfather became one of Europe's biggest industrialists, are today captains of industry. Everyone is free to change his status. That is the difference between the status system and the capitalist system of economic freedom, in which everyone has only himself to blame if he does not reach the position he wants to reach.

The most famous industrialist of the twentieth century up to now is Henry Ford. He started with a few hundred dollars which he had borrowed from his friends, and within a very short time he developed one of the most important big business firms of the world. And one can discover hundreds of such cases every day.

Every day, the *New York Times* prints long notices of people who have died. If you read these biographies, you may come across the name of an eminent businessman, who started out as a seller of newspapers at street corners in New York. Or he started as an office boy, and at his death he is the president of the same banking firm where he started on the lowest rung of the ladder. Of course, not all people can attain these positions. Not all people *want* to attain them. There are people who are more interested in other problems and, for these people, other ways are open today which were not open in the days of feudal society, in the ages of the status society.

The socialist system, however, *forbids* this fundamental freedom to choose one's own career. Under socialist conditions, there is only one economic authority, and it has the right to determine all matters concerning production.

One of the characteristic features of our day is that people use many names for the same thing. One synonym for socialism and communism is "planning." If people speak of "planning" they mean, of course, *central* planning, which means *one plan made by the government*—one plan that prevents planning by anyone except the government.

A British lady, who also is a member of the Upper House, wrote a book entitled *Plan or No Plan*, a book which was quite popular around the world. What does the title of her book mean? When she says "plan," she means only the type of plan envisioned by Lenin and Stalin and their successors, the type which governs all the activities of all the people of a nation. Thus, this lady means a central plan which excludes all the personal plans that individuals may have. Her title *Plan or No Plan* is therefore an illusion, a deception; the alternative is not a central plan or no plan, it is *the total plan* of a central governmental authority *or freedom* for individuals to make their own plans, to do their own planning. The individual plans his life, every day, changing his daily plans whenever he will.

The free man plans daily for his needs; he says, for example: "Yesterday I planned to work all my life in Cordoba." Now he learns about better conditions in Buenos Aires and changes his plans, saying: "Instead of working in Cordoba, I want to go to Buenos Aires." And that is what freedom means. It may be that he is mistaken, it may be that his going to Buenos Aires will turn out to have been a mistake. Conditions may have been better for him in Cordoba, but he himself made his plans.

Under government planning, he is like a soldier in an army. The soldier in the army does not have the right to choose his garrison, to choose the place where he will serve. He has to obey orders. And the socialist system— as Karl Marx, Lenin, and all socialist leaders knew and admitted—is the transfer of army rule to the whole production system. Marx spoke of "industrial armies," and

Lenin called for "the organization of everything—the postoffice, the factory, and other industries, according to the model of the army".

Therefore, in the socialist system everything depends on the wisdom, the talents, and the gifts of those people who form the supreme authority. That which the supreme dictator—or his committee—does *not* know, is not taken into account. But the knowledge which mankind has accumulated in its long history is not acquired by everyone; we have accumulated such an enormous amount of scientific and technological knowledge over the centuries that it is humanly impossible for one individual to know all these things, even though he be a most gifted man.

And people are different, they are unequal. They always will be. There are some people who are more gifted in one subject and less in another one. And there are people who have the gift to find new paths, to change the trend of knowledge. In capitalist societies, technological progress and economic progress are gained through such people. If a man has an idea, he will try to find a few people who are clever enough to realize the value of his idea. Some capitalists, who dare to look into the future, who realize the possible consequences of such an idea, will start to put it to work. Other people, at first, may say: "They are fools"; but they will stop saying so when they discover that this enterprise, which they called foolish, is flourishing, and that people are happy to buy its products.

Under the Marxian system, on the other hand, the supreme government body must first be convinced of the value of such an idea before it can be pursued and developed. This can be a very difficult thing to do, for only the group of people at the head—or the supreme dictator

himself—has the power to make decisions. And if these
people—because of laziness or old age, or because they
are not very bright and learned—are unable to grasp the
importance of the new idea, then the new project will not
be undertaken.

We can think of examples from military history. Napoleon was certainly a genius in military affairs; he had one
serious problem, however, and his inability to solve that
problem culminated, finally, in his defeat and exile to the
loneliness of St. Helena. Napoleon's problem was:
"How to conquer England?" In order to do that, he
needed a navy to cross the English Channel, and there
were people who told him they had a way to accomplish
that crossing, people who—in an age of sailing ships—
had come up with the new idea of steam ships. But
Napoleon did not understand their proposal.

Then there was Germany's famous *Generalstab*. Before
the First World War, the German general staff was univ-
ersally considered to be unsurpassed in military wisdom.
A similar reputation was held by the staff of General
Foch in France. But neither the Germans nor the
French—who, under the leadership of General Foch,
later defeated the Germans—realized the importance of
aviation for military purposes. The German general staff
said: "Aviation is merely for pleasure, flying is good for
idle people. From a military point of view, only the
Zeppelins are important," and the French general staff
was of the same opinion.

Later, during the period between World War I and
World War II, there was a general in the United States
who was convinced that aviation would be very important in the next war. But all other experts in the United
States were against him. He could not convince them. If
you have to convince a group of people who are not

directly dependent on the solution of a problem, you will never succeed. This is true also of noneconomic problems.

There have been painters, poets, writers, composers, who complained that the public did not acknowledge their work and caused them to remain poor. The public may certainly have had poor judgment, but when these artists said: "The government ought to support great artists, painters, and writers," they were very much in the wrong. Whom should the government entrust with the task of deciding whether a newcomer is really a great painter or not? It would have to rely on the judgment of the critics, and the professors of the history of art who are always looking back into the past yet who very rarely have shown the talent to discover new genius. This is the great difference between a system of "planning" and a system in which everyone can plan and act for himself.

It is true, of course, that great painters and great writers have often had to endure great hardships. They might have succeeded in their art, but not always in getting money. Van Gogh was certainly a great painter. He had to suffer unbearable hardship and, finally, when he was thirty-seven years old, he committed suicide. In all his life he sold only *one painting*, and the buyer of it was his cousin. Apart from this one sale, he lived from the money of his brother, who was not an artist nor a painter. But van Gogh's brother understood a painter's needs. Today you cannot buy a van Gogh for less than a hundred or two hundred thousand dollars.

Under a socialist system, van Gogh's fate might have been different. Some government official would have asked some well-known painters (whom van Gogh certainly would not have regarded as artists at all) whether this young man, half or completely crazy, was really a painter worthy to be supported. And they without a doubt, would have answered: "No, he is not a painter; he is not an artist; he is just a man who wastes paint;" and they would have sent him into a milk factory or into a home for the insane. Therefore all this enthusiasm in favor of socialism by the rising generation of painters, poets, musicians, journalists, actors, is based on an *illusion*. I mention this because these groups are among the most fanatical supporters of the socialist idea.

When it comes to choosing between socialism and capitalism as an economic system, the problem is somewhat different. The authors of socialism never suspected that modern industry, and all the operations of modern business, are based on calcuation. Engineers are by no means the only ones who make plans on the basis of calculations, businessmen also must do so. And businessmen's calculations are all based on the fact that, in the market economy, the money prices of goods inform not only the consumer, they also provide vital information to businessmen about the factors of production, the main function of the market being not merely to determine the cost of the *last* part of the process of production and transfer of goods to the hands of the consumer, but the cost of those steps leading up to it. The whole market system is bound up with the fact that there is a mentally calculated division of labor between the various businessmen who vie with each other in bidding for the factors of production—the raw material the machines, the instruments—and for the human factor of production; the wages paid to labor. This sort of calculation by the businessman cannot be accomplished in the absence of prices supplied by the market.

At the very instant you abolish the market—which is what the socialists would like to do—you render useless all the computations and calculations of the engineers and technologists; the technologists can give you a great number of projects which, from the point of view of the natural sciences, are equally feasible, but it takes the market-based *calculations* of the businessman to make clear which of those projects is the most advantageous, from the *economic* point of view.

The problem with which I am dealing here is the fundamental issue of capitalistic economic calculation as opposed to socialism. The fact is that economic calculation, and therefore all technological planning, is possible only if there are money prices, not only for consumer goods but also for the factors of production. This means there has to be a market for all raw materials, for all half-finished goods, for all tools and machines, and for all kinds of human labor and human services.

When this fact was discovered, the socialists did not know how to respond. For 150 years they had said: "All the evils in the world come from the fact that there are markets and market prices. We want to abolish the market and with it, of course, the market economy, and substitute for it a system without prices and without markets." They wanted to abolish what Marx called the "commodity character" of commodities and of labor.

When faced with this new problem, the authors of socialism , having no answer, finally said: "We will not abolish the market altogether; we will pretend that a market exists; we will play market, like children who play school." But everyone knows that when children *play* school, they do not learn anything. It is just an exercise, a game, and you can "play" at many things.

This is a very difficult and complicated problem and in order to deal with it in full one needs a little more time than I have here. I have explained it in detail in my writings. In six lectures I cannot enter into an analysis of all its aspects, therefore, I want to advise you, if you are interested in the fundamental problem of the impossibility of calculation and planning under socialism, read my book "*Human Action*", which is available in an excellent Spanish translation.

But read other books, too, like the book of the Norwegian economist Trygve Hoff, who wrote on economic calculation. And if you do not want to be one-sided, I recommend that you read the highly-regarded socialist book on this subject by the eminent Polish economist Oscar Lange, who at one time was a professor at an American university, then became a Polish ambassador, and later returned to Poland.

You will probably ask me: "What about Russia? How do the Russians handle this question?" This changes the problem. The Russians operate their socialistic system within a world in which there are prices for all the factors of production, for all raw materials, for everything. They can therefore employ, for their planning, the *foreign* prices of the world market. And because there are certain differences between conditions in Russia and those in United States, the result is very often that the Russians consider something to be justified and advisable—from their economic point of view—the Americans would not consider economically justifiable at all.

The "Soviet experiment," as it was called, does not prove anything. It does not tell us anything about the fundamental problem of socialism, the problem of calculation. But are we entitled to speak of it as an experiment? I do not believe there is such a thing as a scientific experiment in the field of human action and economics. You cannot make laboratory experiments in the field of human action because a scientific experiment requires that you do the same thing under various conditions, or that you maintain the same conditions, changing perhaps only one factor. For instance, if you inject into a cancerous animal some experimental medication, the result may be that the cancer will disappear. You can test this with various animals of the same kind which suffer from the same malignancy. If you treat some of them with the new method and do not treat the rest, then you can compare the result. You cannot do this within the field of human action. There are no laboratory experiments in human action.

The so-called Soviet "experiment" merely shows that the standard of living is incomparably lower in Soviet Russia than it is in the country that is considered, by the whole world, as the paragon of capitalism: the United States.

Of course, if you tell this to a socialist, he will say: "Things are wonderful in Russia." And you tell him: "They may be wonderful, but the average standard of living is much lower." Then he will answer: "Yes, but remember how terrible it was for the Russians under the tsars and how terrible a war we had to fight."

I do not want to enter into discussion of whether this is or is not a correct explanation, but if you deny that the conditions are the same, you deny that it was an experiment. You must then say this (which would be much more correct): "Socialism in Russia has not brought about an improvement in the conditions of the average man which can be compared with the improvement of conditions, during the same period, in the United States."

In the United States you hear of something new, of some improvement, almost every week. These are improvements that business has generated, because thousands and thousands of business people are trying day and night to find some new product which satisfies the consumer better or is less expensive to produce, or better *and* less expensive than the existing products. They do not do this out of altruism, they do it because they want to make money. And the effect is that you have an improvement in the standard of living in the United States which is almost miraculous, when compared with the conditions that existed fifty or a hundred years ago. But in Soviet Russia, where you do not have such a system, you do not have a comparable improvement. So those people who tell us that we ought to adopt the Soviet system are badly mistaken.

There is something else that should be mentioned. The American consumer, the individual, is both a buyer and a boss. When you leave a store in America, you may find a sign saying: "Thank you for your patronage. Please come again." But when you go into a shop in a totalitarian country—be it in present-day Russia, or in Germany as it was under the regime of Hitler—the shopkeeper tells you: "You have to be thankful to the great leader for giving you this."

In socialist countries, it is not the seller who has to be grateful, it is the buyer. The citizen is *not* the boss; the boss is the Central Committee, the Central Office. Those socialist committees and leaders and dictators are supreme, and the people simply have to obey them.

3rd Lecture

Interventionism

A famous, very often quoted phrase says: "That government is best, which governs least." I do not believe this to be a correct description of the functions of a good government. Government ought to do all the things for which it is needed and for which it was established. Government ought to protect the individuals within the country against the violent and fraudulent attacks of gangsters, and it should defend the country against foreign enemies. These are the functions of government within a free system, within the system of the market economy.

Under socialism, of course, the government is totalitarian, and there is nothing outside its sphere and its jurisdiction. But in the market economy the main task of the government is to protect the smooth functioning of the market economy against fraud or violence from within and from outside the country.

People who do not agree with this definition of the functions of government may say: "This man hates the government." Nothing could be farther from the truth. If I should say that gasoline is a very useful liquid, useful for many purposes, but that I would nevertheless not drink gasoline because I think that would not be the right use for it, I am not an enemy of gasoline, and I do not hate gasoline. I only say that gasoline is very useful for certain purposes, but not fit for other purposes. If I say it is the government's duty to arrest murderers and other criminals, but not its duty to run the railroads or to spend money for useless things, then I do not hate the government by declaring that it is fit to do certain things but not fit to do other things.

It has been said that under present-day conditions we no longer have a free market economy. Under present-day conditions we have something called the "mixed economy." And for evidence of our "mixed economy," people point to the many enterprises which are operated and owned by the government. The economy is mixed, people say, because there are, in many countries, certain institutions—like the telephone, telegraph, and railroads—which are owned and operated by the government.

That some of these institutions and enterprises are operated by the government is certainly true. But this fact alone does *not* change the character of our economic system. It does not even mean there is a "little socialism" within the otherwise nonsocialist, free market economy. For the government, in operating these enterprises, is subject to the supremacy of the market, which means it is subject to the supremacy of the consumers. The government—if it operates, let us say, post offices or railroads—has to hire people who have to work in these enterprises. It also has to buy the raw materials and other things that are needed for the conduct of these enterprises. And on the other hand, it "sells" these services or commodities to the public. Yet, even though it operates these institutions using the methods of the free economic system, the result, as a rule, is a deficit. The government, however, is in a position to finance such a deficit—at least the members of the government and of the ruling party believe so.

It is certainly different for an individual. The individual's power to operate something with a deficit is very limited. If the deficit is not very soon eliminated, and if the enterprise does not become profitable (or at least show that no further deficit and losses are being incurred), the individual goes bankrupt and the enterprise must come to an end.

But for the government, conditions are different. The government can run at a deficit, because it has the power to *tax* people. And if the taxpayers are prepared to pay higher taxes in order to make it possible for the government to operate an enterprise at a loss—that is, in a less efficient way than it would be done by a private institution—and if the public will accept this loss, then of course the enterprise will continue.

In recent years, governments have increased the number of nationalized institutions and enterprises in most countries to such an extent that the deficits have grown far beyond the amount that could be collected in taxes from the citizens. What happens then is not the subject of today's lecture. It is inflation, and I shall deal with that tomorrow. I mentioned this only because the mixed economy must not be confused with the problem of *interventionism*, about which I want to talk tonight.

What is interventionism? Interventionism means that the government does not restrict its activity to the preservation of order, or—as people used to say a hundred years ago—to "the production of security." Interventionism means that the government wants to do more. It wants to interfere with market phenomena.

If one objects and says the government should not

interfere with business, people very often answer: "But the government necessarily always interferes. If there are policemen on the street, the government interferes. It interferes with a robber looting a shop or it prevents a man from stealing a car." But when dealing with interventionism and defining what is meant by interventionism, we are speaking about government interference with the market. (That the government and the police are expected to protect the citizens, which includes businessmen, and of course their employees, against attacks on the part of domestic or foreign gangsters, is in fact a normal, necessary expectation of any government. Such protection is not an intervention, for the government's only legitimate function is, precisely, to produce security.)

What we have in mind when we talk about interventionism is the government's desire to do *more* than prevent assaults and fraud. Interventionism means that the government not only fails to protect the smooth functioning of the market economy, but that it interferes with the various market phenomena; it interferes with prices, with wage rates, interest rates, and profits.

The government wants to interfere in order to force businessmen to conduct their affairs in a different way than they would have chosen if they had obeyed only the consumers. Thus, all the measures of interventionism by the government are directed toward restricting the supremacy of consumers. The government wants to arrogate to itself the power, or at least a part of the power, which, in the free market economy, is in the hands of the consumers.

Let us consider one example of interventionism, very popular in many countries and tried again and again by many governments, especially in times of inflation. I refer to price control.

Governments usually resort to price control when they have inflated the money supply and people have begun to complain about the resulting rise in prices. There are many famous historical examples of price control methods that failed, but I shall refer to only two of them because, in both these cases, the governments were really very energetic in enforcing or trying to enforce their price controls.

The first famous example is the case of the Roman Emperor Diocletian, very well-known as the last of those Roman emperors who persecuted the Christians. The Roman emperor in the second part of the third century had only one financial method, and this was currency debasement. In those primitive ages, before the invention of the printing press, even inflation was, let us say, primitive. It involved debasement of the coinage, especially the silver. The government mixed more and more copper into the silver until the color of the silver coins was changed and the weight was reduced considerably. The result of this coinage debasement and the associated increase in the quantity of money was an increase in prices, followed by an edict to control prices. And Roman emperors were not very mild when they enforced a law; they did not consider death too mild a punishment for a man who had asked for a higher price. They enforced price control, but they failed to maintain the society. The result was the disintegration of the Roman Empire and the system of the division of labor.

Then, 1500 years later, the same currency debasement took place during the French Revolution. But this time a different method was used. The technology for producing money was considerably improved. It was no longer necessary for the French to resort to debasement of the coinage: they had the printing press. And the printing press was very efficient. Again, the result was an unprecedented rise in prices. But in the French Revolution maximum prices were not enforced by the same method of capital punishment which the Emperor Diocletian had used. There had also been an improvement in the technique of killing citizens. You all remember the famous Doctor J. I. Guillotin (1738-1814), who invented the guillotine. Despite the guillotine the French also failed with their laws of maximum price. When Robespierre himself was carted off to the guillotine the people shouted, "There goes the dirty Maximum."

I wanted to mention this, because people often say: "What is needed in order to make price control effective and efficient is merely more brutality and more energy." Now certainly, Diocletian was very brutal, and so was the French Revolution. Nevertheless, price control measures in both ages failed entirely.

Now let us analyze the reasons for this failure. The government hears people complain that the price of milk has gone up. And milk is certainly very important, especially for the rising generation, for children. Consequently, the government declares a maximum price for milk, a maximum price that is lower than the potential market price would be. Now the government says: "Certainly we have done everything needed in order to make it possible for poor parents to buy as much milk as they need to feed their children."

But what happens? On the one hand, the lower price of milk increases the demand for milk; people who could not afford to buy milk at a higher price are now able to buy it at the lower price which the government has decreed. And on the other hand some of the producers, those producers of milk who are producing at the highest cost—that is, the marginal producers—are now suffering losses, because the price which the government has decreed is lower than their costs. This is the important point in the market economy.

The private entrepreneur, the private producer, cannot take losses in the long run. And as he cannot take losses in milk, he restricts the production of milk for the market. He may sell some of his cows for the slaughter house, or instead of milk he may sell some products made out of milk, for instance sour cream, butter or cheese.

Thus the government's interference with the price of milk will result in less milk than there was before, and at the same time there will be a greater demand. Some people who are prepared to pay the government-decreed price cannot buy it. Another result will be that anxious people will hurry to be first at the shops. They have to wait outside. The long lines of people waiting at shops always appear as a familiar phenomenon in a city in which the government has decreed maximum prices for commodities that the government considers as important. This has happened everywhere when the price of milk was controlled. This was always prognosticated by economists. Of course, only by sound economists, and their number is not very great. But what is the result of the government's price control? The government is disappointed. It wanted to increase the satisfaction of the milk drinkers. But actually it has dissatisifed them. Before the government interfered, milk was expensive, but people could buy it. Now there is only an insufficient quantity of milk available. Therefore, the total consumption of milk drops. The children are getting less milk, not more. The next measure to which the government now resorts, is rationing. But rationing only means that certain people are privileged and are getting milk while other people are *not* getting any at all. Who gets milk and who does not, of course, is always very arbitrarily determined. One order may determine, for example, that children under four years old should get milk, and that children over four years, or between the age of four and six should get only half the ration which children under four years receive. Whatever the government does, the fact remains, there is only a smaller amount of milk available. Thus people are still more dissatisfied than they were before. Now the government asks the milk producers (because the government does not have enough imagination to find out for itself): "Why do you not produce the same amount of milk you produced before?" The government gets the answer: "We cannot do it, since the costs of production are higher than the maximum price which the government has established." Now the government studies the costs of the various items of production, and it discovers one of the items is fodder.

"Oh," says the government, "the same control we applied to milk we will now apply to fodder. We will determine a maximum price for fodder, and then you will be able to feed your cows at a lower price, at a lower expenditure. Then everything will be all right; you will be able to produce more milk and you will sell more milk."

But what happens now? The same story repeats itself with fodder, and as you can understand, for the same reasons. The production of fodder drops and the government is again faced with a dilemma. So the government arranges new hearings, to find out what is wrong with fodder production. And it gets an explanation from the producers of fodder precisely like the one it got from the milk producers. So the government must go a step farther, since it does not want to abandon the principle of price control. It determines maximum prices for producers' goods which are necessary for the production of fodder. And the same story happens again.

The government at the same time starts controlling not only milk, but also eggs, meat, and other necessities. And every time the government gets the same result, everywhere the consequence is the same. Once the government fixes a maximum price for consumer goods, it has to go farther back to producers' goods, and limit the prices of the producers' goods required for the production of the price-controlled consumer goods. And so the government, having started with only a few price controls, goes farther and farther back in the process of production, fixing maximum prices for all kinds of producers' goods, including of course the price of labor, because without wage control, the government's "cost control" would be meaningless.

Moreover, the government cannot limit its interference into the market to only those things which it views as vital necessities, like milk, butter, eggs, and meat. It must necessarily include luxury goods, because if it did not limit *their* prices, capital and labor would abandon the production of vital necessities and would turn to producing those things which the government considers unnecessary luxury goods. Thus, the isolated interference with one or a few prices of consumer goods always brings about effects—and this is important to realize— which are even *less* satisfactory than the conditions that prevailed before: before the government interfered, milk and eggs were expensive; after the government interference they began to disappear from the market.

The government considered those items to be so important that it interfered; it wanted to increase the quantity and improve the supply. The result was the opposite: the isolated interference brought about a condition which—from the point of view of the government—is even *more* undesirable than the previous state of affairs which the government wanted to alter. And as the government goes farther and farther, it will finally arrive at a point where all prices, all wage rates, all interest rates, in short everything in the whole economic system, is determined by the government. And this, clearly, is *socialism*.

What I have told you here, this schematic and theoretical explanation, is precisely what happened in those countries which tried to enforce a maximum price control, where governments were stubborn enough to go step by step until they came to the end. This happened in the First World War, in Germany and England.

Let us analyze the situation in both countries. Both countries experienced inflation. Prices went up, and the two governments imposed price controls. Starting with a few prices, starting with only milk and eggs, they had to go farther and farther. The longer the war went on, the more inflation was generated. And after three years of war, the Germans—systematically as always— elaborated a great plan. They called it the *Hindenburg Plan*: everything in Germany considered to be good by the government at that time was named after Hindenburg.

The Hindenburg Plan meant that the whole German economic system should be controlled by the government: prices, wages, profits...everything. And the bureaucracy immediately began to put this into effect. But before they had finished, the debacle came: the German empire broke down, the entire bureaucratic apparatus disappeared, the revolution brought its bloody results—things came to an end.

In England they started in the same way, but after a time, in the spring of 1917, the United States entered the war and supplied the British with sufficient quantities of everything. Therefore the road to socialism, the road to serfdom, was interrupted.

Before Hitler came to power, Chancellor Brüning again introduced price control in Germany for the usual reasons. Hitler enforced it, even before the war started. For, in Hitler's Germany, there was no private enterprise or private initiative. In Hitler's Germany there was a system of socialism which differed from the Russian system only to the extent that the *terminology and labels* of the free economic system were still retained. There still existed "private enterprises," as they were called. But the owner was no longer an entrepreneur, the owner was called a "shop manager" (Betriebsführer).

The whole of Germany was organized in a hierarchy of führers; there was the Highest Führer, Hitler of course, and then there were führers down to the many hierarchies of smaller führers. And the head of an enterprise was the *Betriebsführer*. And the workers of the enterprise were named by a word that, in the Middle Ages, had signified the retinue of a feudal lord: the *Gefolgschaft*. And all of these people had to obey the orders issued by an institution which had a terribly long name: *Reichsführerwirtschaftsministerium*, at the head of which was the well-known fat man, named Goering, adorned with jewelry and medals.

And from this body of ministers with the long name came all the orders to every enterprise: what to produce, in what quantity, where to get the raw materials and what to pay for them, to whom to sell the products and at what prices to sell them. The workers got the order to work in a definite factory, and they received wages which the government decreed. The whole economic system was now regulated in every detail by the government.

The *Betriebsführer* did not have the right to take the profits for himself; he received what amounted to a salary, and if he wanted to get more he would, for example, say: "I am very sick, I need an operation immediately, and the operation will cost 500 Marks," then he had to ask the führer of the district (the *Gauführer* or *Gauleiter*) whether he had the right to take out more than the salary which was given to him. The prices were no longer prices, the wages were no longer wages, they were all quantitative *terms* in a system of socialism.

Now let me tell you how that system broke down. One day, after years of fighting, the foreign armies arrived in Germany. They tried to preserve this government-directed economic system, but the brutality of Hitler would have been necessary to preserve it and, without this, it did not work.

And while this was going on in Germany, Great Britain—during the Second World War—did precisely what Germany did: starting with the price control of some commodities only, the British government began step by step (in the same way Hitler had done in peacetime, even before the start of the war) to control more and more of the economy until, by the time the war ended, they had reached something that was almost pure socialism.

Great Britain was not brought to socialism by the Labour government which was established in 1945. Great Britain became socialist *during* the war, through the government of which Sir Winston Churchill was the prime minister. The Labour government simply retained the system of socialism which the government of Sir Winston Churchill had already introduced. And this in spite of great resistance by the people.

The nationalizations in Great Britain did not mean very much; the nationalization of the Bank of England was merely nominal, because the Bank of England was already under the complete control of the government. And it was the same with the nationalization of the railroads and the steel industry. The "war socialism," as it was called—meaning the system of interventionism proceeding step by step—had already virtually nationalized the system.

The difference between the German and British systems was not important since the people who operated them had been appointed by the government and in both cases they had to obey the government's orders in every respect. As I said before, the system of the German Nazis retained the labels and terms of the capitalistic free market economy. But they meant something very different: there were now only government decrees.

This was also true for the British system. When the Conservative party in Britain was returned to power, some of those controls were removed. In Great Britain we now have attempts from one side to retain controls and from the other side to abolish them. (But one must not forget that, in England, conditions are very different from conditions in Russia.) The same is true for other countries which depend on the importation of food and raw materials and therefore have to export manufactured goods. For countries depending heavily on export trade, a system of government control simply does not work.

Thus, as far as there is economic freedom left (and there is still substantial freedom in some countries, such as Norway, England, Sweden), it exists because of the *necessity to retain export trade*. Earlier, I chose the example of milk, not because I have a special preference for milk, but because practically all governments—or most of them—in recent decades, have regulated milk, egg or butter prices.

I want to refer, in a few words, to another example, and that is rent control. If the government controls rents, one result is that people who would otherwise have moved from bigger apartments to smaller ones when their family conditions changed, will no longer do so. For example, consider parents whose children left home when they came into their twenties, married or went into other cities to work. Such parents used to change their apartments and take smaller and cheaper ones. This necessity disappeared when rent controls were imposed.

In Vienna, Austria, in the early twenties, where rent control was well-establshed, the amount of money that the landlord received for an average apartment under rent control was not more than twice the price of a ticket for a ride on the city-owned street cars. You can imagine that people did not have any incentive to change their apartments. And, on the other hand, there was no construction of new houses. Similar conditions prevailed in the United States after the Second World War and are continuing in many cities to this day.

One of the main reasons why many cities in the United States are in such great financial difficulty is that they have rent control and a resulting shortage of housing. So the government has spent billions for the building of new houses. But why was there such a housing shortage? The housing shortage developed for the same reasons that brought milk shortages when there was milk price control. That means: *when the government interferes with the market, it is more and more driven towards socialism.*

And this is the answer to those people who say: "We are not socialists, we do not want the government to control everything. We realize this is bad. But why should not the government interfere a little bit with the market? Why shouldn't the government do away with some things which we do not like?"

These people talk of a "middle-of-the-road" policy. What they do not see is that the *isolated* interference, which means the interference with only one small part of the economic system, brings about a situation which the government itself—and the people who are asking for government interference—find worse than the conditions they wanted to abolish: the people who are asking for rent control are very angry when they discover there is a shortage of apartments and a shortage of housing.

But this shortage of housing was created precisely by government interference, by the establishment of rents below the level people would have had to pay in a free market.

The idea that there is a *third* system—between socialism and capitalism, as its supporters say—a system as far away from socialism as it is from capitalism but retains the advantages and avoids the disadvantages of each—is pure nonsense. People who believe there is such a mythical system can become really poetic when they praise the glories of interventionism. One can only say they are mistaken. The government interference

which they praise brings about conditions which they
themselves do not like.

One of the problems I will deal with later is *protectionism*. The government tries to isolate the domestic
market from the world market. It introduces tariffs which
raise the domestic price of a commodity above the world
market price, making it possible for domestic producers
to form cartels. The cartels are then attacked by the
government. It then attacks the cartels, declaring: "Under these conditions, anti-cartel legislation is necessary."

This is precisely the situation with most of the European governments. In the United States, there are yet
other reasons for antitrust legislation and the government's campaign against the specter of monopoly.

It is absurd to see the government—which creates by
its own intervention the conditions making possible the
emergence of domestic cartels—point its finger at business, saying: "There are cartels, therefore government
interference with business is necessary." It would be
much simpler to avoid cartels by ending the government's interference with the market—an interference
which makes these cartels possible.

The idea of government interference as a "solution" to
economic problems leads, in every country, to conditions which, at the least, are very unsatisfactory and
often quite chaotic. If the government does not stop in
time, it will bring on socialism.

Nevertheless, government interference with business
is still very popular. As soon as someone does not like
something that happens in the world, he says: "The
government ought to do something about it. What do we
have a government for? The government should do it."
And this is a characteristic remnant of thought from past
ages, of ages *preceding* modern freedom, modern con-

stitutional government, before representative government or modern republicanism.

For centuries there was the doctrine—maintained and accepted by everyone—that a king, an anointed king, was the messenger of God; he had more wisdom than his subjects, and he had supernatural powers. As recently as the beginning of the nineteenth century, people suffering from certain diseases expected to be cured by the royal touch, by the hand of the king. Doctors were usually better; nevertheless, they had their patients try the king.

This doctrine of the superiority of a paternal government, of the supernatural and superhuman powers of the hereditary kings gradually disappeared—or at least we thought so. But it came back again. There was a German professor named Werner Sombart (I knew him very well), who was known the world over, who was an honorary doctor of many universities and an honorary member of the American Economic Association. That professor wrote a book, which is available in an English translation, published by the Princeton University Press. It is available also in a French translation, and probably also in Spanish—at least I hope it is available, because then you can check what I am saying. In this book, published in our century, not in the Dark Ages, "Sir" Werner Sombart, a professor of economics, simply says: "The Führer, our Führer"—he means, of course, Hitler—"gets his orders directly from God, the Führer of the Universe."

I spoke of this hierarchy of the führers earlier, and in this hierarchy, I mentioned Hitler as the "Supreme Führer"...But there is, according to Werner Sombart, a still higher Führer, God, the Führer of the universe. And God, he wrote, gives His orders directly to Hitler. Of

course, Professor Sombart said very modestly: "We do
not know how God communicates with the Führer. But
the fact cannot be denied."

Now, if you hear that such a book can be published in
the German language, the language of a nation which
was once hailed as "the nation of philosophers and
poets," and if you see it translated into English and
French, then you will not be astonished at the fact that
even a little bureaucrat considers himself wiser and better than the citizens and wants to interfere with everything, even though he is only a poor little bureaucrat,
and not the famous Professor Werner Sombart, honorary
member of everything.

Is there a remedy against such happenings? I would
say, yes, there is a remedy. And this remedy is the power
of the citizens; they have to prevent the establishment of
such an autocratic regime that arrogates to itself a higher
wisdom than that of the average citizen. This is the
fundamental difference between freedom and serfdom.

The socialist nations have arrogated to themselves the
term *democracy*. The Russians call their own system a
People's Democracy; they probably maintain that the
people are represented in the person of the dictator. I
think that *one* dictator, here in Argentina, was given a
good answer. Let us hope that all other dictators, in other
nations, will be accorded a similar response.

Inflation

If the supply of caviar were as plentiful as the supply of potatoes, the price of caviar—that is, the exchange ratio between caviar and money or caviar and other commodities—would change considerably. In that case, one could obtain caviar at a much smaller sacrifice than is required today. Likewise, if the quantity of money is increased, the purchasing power of the monetary unit decreases, and the quantity of goods that can be obtained for one unit of this money decreases also.

When, in the sixteenth century, American resources of gold and silver were discovered and exploited, enormous quantities of the precious metals were transported to Europe. The result of this increase in the quantity of money was a general tendency toward an upward movement of prices. In the same way, today, when a government increases the quantity of paper money, the result is that the purchasing power of the monetary unit begins to drop, and so prices rise. This is called *inflation*.

Unfortunately, in the United States, as well as in other countries, some people prefer to attribute the cause of inflation not to an increase in the quantity of money but, rather, to the rise in prices.

However, there has never been any serious argument against the economic interpretation of the relationship between prices and the quantity of money, or the exchange ratio between money and other goods, commodities, and services. Under present day technological conditions there is nothing easier than to manufacture pieces of paper upon which certain monetary amounts are printed. In the United States, where all the notes are of the same size, it does not cost the government more to print a bill of a thousand dollars than it does to print a bill of one dollar. It is purely a printing procedure that requires the same quantity of paper and ink.

In the eighteenth century, when the first attempts were made to issue bank notes and to give these bank notes the quality of legal tender—that is, the right to be honored in exchange transactions in the same way that gold and silver pieces were honored—the governments and nations believed that bankers had some secret knowledge enabling them to produce wealth out of nothing. When the governments of the eighteenth century were in financial difficulties, they thought all they needed was a clever banker at the head of their financial management in order to get rid of all their difficulties.

Some years before the French Revolution, when the royalty of France was in financial trouble, the king of France sought out such a clever banker, and appointed him to a high position. This man was, in every regard, the opposite of the people who, up to that time, had ruled France. First of all he was not a Frenchman, he was a foreigner—a Genevese. Secondly, he was not a member of the aristocracy, he was a simple commoner. And what counted even more in eighteenth century France, he was not a Catholic, but a Protestant. And so Monsieur Necker, the father of the famous Madame de Staël, became the minister of finance, and everyone expected him to solve the financial problems of France. But in spite of the high degree of confidence Monsieur Necker enjoyed, the royal cashbox remained empty— Necker's greatest mistake having been his attempt to finance aid to the American colonists in their war of independence against England *without raising taxes.* That was certainly the wrong way to go about solving France's financial troubles.

There can be no secret way to the solution of the financial problems of a government; if it needs money, it has to obtain the money by taxing its citizens (or, under special conditions, by borrowing it from people who have the money). But many governments, we can even say *most* governments, think there is another method for getting the needed money; simply to print it.

If the government wants to do something beneficial— if, for example, it wants to build a hospital—the way to find the needed money for this project is to tax the citizens and build the hospital out of tax revenues. Then no special "price revolution" will occur, because when the government collects money for the construction of the hospital, the citizens—having paid the taxes—are forced to reduce their spending. The individual taxpayer is forced to restrict either his consumption, his investments or his savings. The government, appearing on the market as a buyer, *replaces* the individual citizen: the citizen buys less, but the government buys more. The government, of course, does not always buy the same goods which the citizens would have bought; but on the average there occurs no rise in prices due to the government's construction of a hospital.

I choose this example of a hospital precisely because people sometimes say: "It makes a difference whether the government uses its money for good or for bad purposes." I want to assume that the government *always* uses the money which it has printed for the best possible purposes—purposes with which we all agree. For it is not the *way* in which the money is spent, it is the way in which the government *obtains* this money that brings about those consequences we call inflation and which most people in the world today do not consider as beneficial.

For example, without inflating, the government could use the tax-collected money for hiring new employees or for raising the salaries of those who are already in government service. Then these people, whose salaries have been increased, are in a position to buy more. When the government taxes the citizens and uses this money to increase the salaries of government employees, the taxpayers have less to spend, but the government employees have more. Prices in general will not increase.

But if the government does not use tax money for this purpose, if it uses freshly printed money instead, it means that there will be people who now have more money while all other people still have as much as they had before. So those who received the newly-printed money will be competing with those people who were buyers before. And since there are no more commodities than there were previously, but there *is* more money on the market—and since there are now people who can buy more today than they could have bought yesterday—there will be an additional demand for that same quantity of goods. Therefore prices will tend to go up. This cannot be avoided, no matter what the use of this newly-issued money will be.

And most importantly, this tendency for prices to go up will develop step by step; it is not a general upward movement of what has been called the "price level." The metaphorical expression "price level" must never be used.

When people talk of a "price level," they have in mind the image of a level of a liquid which goes up or down according to the increase or decrease in its quantity, but which, like a liquid in a tank, always rises evenly. But with prices, there is no such thing as a "level." Prices do not change to the same extent at the same time. There are always prices that are changing more rapidly, rising or falling more rapidly than other prices. There is a reason for this.

Consider the case of the government employee who received the new money added to the money supply. People do not buy today precisely the same commodities and in the same quantities as they did yesterday. The additional money which the government has printed and introduced into the market is not used for the purchase of *all* commodities and services. It is used for the purchase of certain commodities, the prices of which will rise, while other commodities will still remain at the prices that prevailed before the new money was put on the market. Therefore, when inflation starts, different groups within the population are affected by this inflation, in different ways. Those groups who get the new money first, gain a temporary benefit.

When the government inflates in order to wage a war, it has to buy munitions, and the first to get the additional money are the munition industries and the workers within these industries. These groups are now in a very favorable position. They have higher profits and higher wages; their business is moving. Why? Because they were the first to receive the additional money. And having now more money at their disposal, they are buying.

And they are buying from other people who are manufacturing and selling the commodities that these munition makers want.

These other people form a second group. And this
second group considers inflation to be very good for
business. Why not? Isn't it wonderful to sell more? For
example, the owner of a restaurant in the neighborhood
of a munitions factory says: "It is really marvelous! The
munition workers have more money; there are many
more of them now than before; they are all patronizing
my restaurant; I am very happy about it." He does not
see any reason to feel otherwise.

The situation is this: those people to whom the money
comes first now have a higher income, and they can still
buy many commodities and services at prices which cor-
respond to the previous state of the market, to the condition that existed on the eve of inflation. Therefore, they
are in a very favorable position. And thus inflation con-
tinues step by step, from one group of the population to
another. And all those to whom the additional money
comes at the early state of inflation are benefited because
they are buying some things at prices still corresponding
to the previous stage of the exchange ratio between
money and commodities.

But there are other groups in the population to whom
this additional money comes much, much later. These
people are in an *unfavorable* position. Before the additional money comes to them they are forced to pay higher
prices than they paid before for some—or for practically
all—of the commodities they wanted to purchase, while
their income has remained the same, or has not increased
proportionately with prices.

Consider for instance a country like the United States
during the Second World War; on the one hand, inflation

at that time favored the munitions workers, the munition industries, the manufacturers of guns, while on the other hand it worked against other groups of the population. And the ones who suffered the greatest disadvantages from inflation were the teachers and the ministers.

As you know, a minister is a very modest person who serves God and must not talk too much about money. Teachers, likewise, are dedicated persons who are supposed to think more about educating the young than about their salaries. Consequently, the teachers and ministers were among those who were most penalized by inflation, for the various schools and churches were the last to realize that they must raise salaries. When the church elders and the school corporations finally discovered that, after all one should also raise the salaries of those dedicated people, the earlier losses they had suffered still remained.

For a long time, they had to buy less than they did before, to cut down their consumption of better and more expensive foods, and to restrict their purchase of clothing—because prices had already adjusted upward, while their income, their salaries, had not yet been raised. (This situation has changed considerably today, at least for teachers.)

There are therefore always different groups in the population being affected differently by inflation. For some of them, inflation is not so bad; they even ask for a continuation of it, because they are the first to profit from it. We will see, in the next lecture, how this unevenness in the consequences of inflation vitally affects the politics that lead toward inflation.

Under these changes brought about by inflation, we have groups who are favored and groups who are directly profiteering. I do not use the term "profiteering" as a reproach to these people, for if there is someone to blame, it is the government that established the inflation. And there are always people who *favor* inflation, because they realize what is going on sooner than other people do. Their special profits are due to the fact that there will necessarily be unevenness in the process of inflation.

The government may think that inflation—as a method of raising funds—is better than taxation, which is always unpopular and difficult. In many rich and great nations, legislators have often discussed, for months and months, the various forms of new taxes that were necessary because the parliament had decided to increase expenditures. Having discussed various methods of getting the money by taxation, they finally decided that perhaps it was better to do it by inflation.

But of course, the word "inflation" was not used. The politician in power who proceeds toward inflation does not announce: "I am proceeding toward inflation." The technical methods employed to achieve the inflation are so complicated that the average citizen does not realize inflation has begun.

During one of the biggest inflations in history, in the German Reich after the First World War, the inflation was not so momentous during the war. It was the inflation *after* the war that brought about the catastrophe. The government did not say: "We are proceeding toward inflation." The government simply borrowed money very indirectly from the central bank. The government did not have to ask how the central bank would find and deliver the money. The central bank simply printed it.

Today the techniques for inflation are complicated by the fact that there is checkbook money. It involves another technique, but the result is the same. With the stroke of a pen, the government creates *fiat* money, thus increasing the quantity of money and credit. The government simply issues the order, and the fiat money is there.

The government does not care, at first, that some people will be losers, it does not care that prices will go up. The legislators say: "This is a wonderful system!" But this wonderful system has one fundamental weakness: it cannot last. If inflation could go on forever, there would be no point in telling governments they should not inflate. But the certain fact about inflation is that, sooner or later, it must come to an end. It is a policy that cannot last.

In the long run, inflation comes to an end with the breakdown of the currency—to a catastrophe, to a situation like the one in Germany in 1923. On August 1, 1914, the value of the dollar was four marks and twenty pfennigs. Nine years and three months later, in November 1923, the dollar was pegged at 4.2 billion marks. In other words, the mark was worth nothing. It no longer had *any* value.

Some years ago, a famous author wrote: "In the long run we are all dead." This is certainly true, I am sorry to say. But the question is, how short or long will the short run be? In the eighteenth century there was a famous lady, Madame de Pompadour, who is credited with the dictum: "Après nous le déluge" ("After us will come the flood"). Madame de Pompadour was happy enough to die in the short run. But her successor in office, Madame du Barry, outlived the short run and was beheaded in the long run. For many people the "long run" quickly becomes the "short run"—and the longer inflation goes on the sooner the "short run".

How long can the short run last? How long can a central bank continue an inflation? Probably as long as people are convinced that the government, sooner or later, but certainly not too late, will stop printing money and thereby stop decreasing the value of each unit of money.

When people no longer believe this, when they realize that the government will go on and on without any intention of stopping, then they begin to understand that prices tomorrow will be higher than they are today. Then they begin buying at any price, causing prices to go up to such heights that the monetary system breaks down.

I refer to the case of Germany, which the whole world was watching. Many books have described the events of that time. (Although I am no German, but an Austrian, I saw everything from the inside: in Austria, conditions were not very different from those in Germany; nor were they much different in many other European countries.) For several years, the German people believed that their inflation was just a temporary affair, that it would soon come to an end. They believed it for almost nine years, until the summer of 1923. Then, finally, they began to doubt. As the inflation continued, people thought it wiser to buy everything available, instead of keeping money in their pockets. Furthermore, they reasoned that one should not give loans of money, but on the contrary, that it was a very good idea to be a debtor. Thus inflation continued feeding on itself.

And it went on in Germany until exactly August 28, 1923. The masses had believed inflation money to be real money, but then they found out that conditions had changed. At the end of the German inflation, in the fall of 1923, the German factories paid their workers every morning in advance for the day. And the workingman who came to the factory with his wife, handed his wages—all the millions he got—over to her immediately. And the lady immediately went to a shop to buy something, no matter what. She realized what most people knew at that time—that overnight, from one day to another, the mark lost 50% of its purchasing power. Money, like chocolate on a hot oven, was melting in the pockets of the people. This last phase of German inflation did not last long; after a few days, the whole nightmare was over: the mark was valueless and a new currency had to be established.

Lord Keynes, the same man who said that in the long run we are all dead, was one of a long line of inflationist authors of the twentieth century. They all wrote against the gold standard. When Keynes attacked the gold standard, he called it a "barbarous relic." And most people today consider it ridiculous to speak of a return to the gold standard. In the United States, for instance, you are considered to be more or less a dreamer if you say: "Sooner or later, the United States will have to return to the gold standard."

Yet the gold standard has one tremendous virtue: the quantity of the money supply, under the gold standard, is independent of the policies of governments and political parties. This is its advantage. It is a form of protection against spendthrift governments. If, under the gold standard, a government is asked to spend money for something new, the minister of finance can say: "And where do I get the money? Tell me, first, how I will find the money for this additional expenditure."

Under an inflationary system, nothing is simpler for the politicians to do than to order the government printing office to provide as much money as they need for their projects. Under a gold standard, sound government has a much better chance; its leaders can say to the people and to the politicians: "We can't do it unless we increase taxes."

But under inflationary conditions, people acquire the habit of looking upon the government as an institution with limitless means at its disposal: the state, the government, can do anything. If, for instance, the nation wants a new highway system, the government is expected to build it. But where will the government get the money?

One could say that in the United States today—and even in the past, under McKinley—the Republican party was more or less in favor of sound money and of the gold standard, and the Democratic party was in favor of inflation. Of course not a paper inflation, but of silver.

It was, however, a Democratic president of the United States, President Cleveland, who at the end of the 1880s vetoed a decision of Congress, to give a small sum— about $10,000—to help a community that had suffered some disaster. And President Cleveland justified his veto by writing: "While it is the duty of the citizens to support the government, it is not the duty of the government to support the citizens." This is something which every statesman should write on the wall of his office to show to people who come asking for money.

I am rather embarrassed by the necessity to simplify these problems. There are so many complex problems in the monetary system, and I would not have written volumes about them if they were as simple as I am describing them here. But the fundamentals are precisely these: if you increase the quantity of money, you bring about the lowering of the purchasing power of the monetary unit. This is what people whose private affairs are unfavorably affected do not like. People who do not benefit from inflation are the ones who complain.

If inflation is bad and if people realize it, why has it become almost a way of life in all countries? Even some of the richest countries suffer from this disease. The United States today is certainly the richest country in the world, with the highest standard of living. But when you travel in the United States, you will discover that there is constant talk about inflation and about the necessity to stop it. But they only talk; they do not act.

To give you some facts: after the First World War, Great Britain returned to the prewar gold parity of the pound. That is, it revalued the pound upward. This increased the purchasing power of every worker's wages. In an unhampered market the nominal *money* wage would have fallen to compensate for this and the workers' *real* wage would not have suffered. We do not have time here to discuss the reasons for this. But the unions in Great Britain were unwilling to accept an adjustment of wage rates to the higher purchasing power of the monetary unit, therefore *real* wages were raised considerably by this monetary measure. This was a serious catastrophe for England, because Great Britain is a predominantly industrial country that has to import its raw materials, half-finished goods, and food stuffs in order to live, and has to export manufactured goods to pay for these imports. With the rise in the international value of the pound, the price of British goods rose on foreign markets and sales and exports declined. Great Britain had, in effect, priced itself out of the world market.

The unions could not be defeated. You know the power of a union today. It has the right, practically the privilege, to resort to violence. And a union order is, therefore, let us say, not less important than a government decree. The government decree is an order for enforcement for which the enforcement apparatus of the government—the police—is ready. You must obey the government decree, otherwise you will have difficulties with the police.

Unfortunately, we have now, in almost all countries all over the world, a second power that is in a position to exercise force: the labor unions. The labor unions determine wages and the strikes to enforce them in the same way in which the government might decree a minimum wage rate. I will not discuss the union question now; I shall deal with it later. I only want to establish that it is the union policy to raise wage rates *above* the level they would have on an unhampered market. As a result, a considerable part of the potential labor force can be employed only by people or industries that are prepared to suffer losses. And, since businesses are not able to keep on suffering losses, they close their doors and people become unemployed. The setting of wage rates above the level they would have on the unhampered market always results in the unemployment of a considerable part of the potential labor force.

In Great Britain, the result of high wage rates enforced by the labor unions was lasting unemployment, prolonged year after year. Millions of workers were unemployed, production figures dropped. Even experts were perplexed. In this situation the British government made a move which it considered an indispensable, emergency measure: it *devalued* its currency.

The result was that the purchasing power of the money wages, upon which the unions had insisted, was no longer the same. The *real* wages, the commodity wages, were reduced. Now the worker could not buy as much as he had been able to buy before, even though the nominal wage rates remained the same. In this way, it was thought, *real* wage rates would return to free market levels and unemployment would disappear.

This measure—devaluation—was adopted by various other countries, by France, the Netherlands, and Belgium. One country even resorted twice to this measure within a period of one year and a half. That country was Czechoslovakia. It was a surreptitious method, let us say, to thwart the power of the unions. You could not call it a real success, however.

After a few years, the people, the workers, even the unions, began to understand what was going on. They came to realize that currency devaluation had reduced their real wages. The unions had the power to oppose this. In many countries they inserted a clause into wage contracts providing that money wages must go up automatically with an increase in prices. This is called *indexing*. The unions became index conscious. So, this method of reducing unemployment that the government of Great Britain started in 1931—which was later adopted by almost all important governments—this method of "solving unemployment" no longer works today.

In 1936, in his *General Theory of Employment, Interest and Money*, Lord Keynes unfortunately elevated this method—those emergency measures of the period between 1929 and 1933—to a *principle*, to a fundamental system of policy. And he justified it by saying, in effect: "Unemployment is bad. If you want unemployment to disappear you must inflate the currency."

He realized very well that wage rates can be too high for the market, that is, too high to make it profitable for an employer to increase his work force, thus too high from the point of view of the total working population, for with wage rates imposed by unions above the market level, only a part of those anxious to earn wages can obtain jobs.

And Keynes said, in effect: "Certainly mass unemployment, prolonged year after year, is a very unsatisfactory condition." But instead of suggesting that wage rates could and should be adjusted to market conditions, he said, in effect: "If one devalues the currency and the workers are not clever enough to realize it, they will not offer resistance against a drop in real wage rates, as long as nominal wage rates remain the same." In other words, Lord Keynes was saying that if a man gets the same amount of sterling today as he got before the currency was devalued, he will not realize that he is, in fact, now getting less.

In old fashioned language, Keynes proposed cheating the workers. Instead of declaring openly that wage rates must be adjusted to the conditions of the market—because, if they are not, a part of the labor force will inevitably remain unemployed—he said, in effect: "Full employment can be reached only if you have inflation. Cheat the workers." The most interesting fact, however, is that when his *General Theory* was published, it was no longer possible to cheat, because people had already become index conscious. But the goal of full employment remained.

What does "full employment" mean? It has to do with the unhampered labor market, which is not manipulated by the unions or by the government. On this market, wage rates for every type of labor tend to reach a level where everybody who wants a job can get one and every employer can hire as many workers as he needs. If there is an increase in the demand for labor, the wage rate will tend to be greater, and if fewer workers are needed, the wage rate will tend to fall.

The only method by which a "full employment" situation can be brought about is by the maintenance of an unhampered labor market. This is valid for every kind of labor and for every kind of commodity.

What does a businessman do who wants to sell a commodity for five dollars a unit? When he cannot sell it at that price, the technical business expression in the United States is, "the inventory does not move." But it *must* move. He cannot retain things because he must buy something new; fashions are changing. So he sells at a lower price. If he cannot sell the merchandise at five dollars, he must sell it at four. If he cannot sell it at four, he must sell it at three. There is no other choice as long as he stays in business. He may suffer losses, but these losses are due to the fact that his anticipation of the market for his product was wrong.

It is the same with the thousands and thousands of young people who come every day from the agricultural districts into the city, trying to earn money. It happens so in every industrial nation. In the United States they come to town with the idea that they should get, say, a hundred dollars a week. This may be impossible. So if a man cannot get a job for a hundred dollars a week, he must try to get a job for ninety or eighty dollars, and perhaps even less. But if he were to say—as the unions do—"one hundred dollars a week or nothing," then he might have to remain unemployed. (Many do not mind being unemployed, because the government pays unemployment benefits—out of special taxes levied on the employers—which are sometimes nearly as high as the wages the man would receive if he were employed.)

Because a certain group of people believes that full

employment can be attained only by inflation, inflation is accepted in the United States. But people are discussing the question: Should we have a sound currency with unemployment, or inflation with full employment? This is in fact a very vicious analysis.

To deal with this problem we must raise the question: How can one improve the condition of the workers and of all other groups of the population? The answer is: by maintaining an unhampered labor market and thus achieving full employment. Our dilemma is, shall the market determine wage rates or shall they be determined by union pressure and compulsion? The dilemma is *not* "shall we have inflation or unemployment?"

This mistaken analysis of the problem is argued in England, in European industrial countries and even in the United States. And some people say: "Now look, even the United States is inflating. Why should we not do it also."

To these people one should answer first of all: "One of the privileges of a rich man is that he can afford to be foolish much longer than a poor man." And this is the situation of the United States. The financial policy of the United States is very bad and is getting worse. Perhaps the United States can afford to be foolish a bit longer than some other countries.

The most important thing to remember is that inflation is not an act of God, that inflation is not a catastrophe of the elements or a disease that comes like the plague. Inflation is a *policy*—a deliberate policy of people who resort to inflation because they consider it to be a lesser evil than unemployment. But the fact is that, in the not very long run, inflation does *not* cure unemployment.

Inflation is a policy. And a policy can be changed. Therefore, there is no reason to give in to inflation. If one regards inflation as an evil, then one has to stop inflating. One has to balance the budget of the government. Of course, public opinion must support this; the intellectuals must help the people to understand. Given the support of public opinion, it is certainly possible for the people's elected representatives to abandon the policy of inflation.

We must remember that, in the long run, we may all be dead and certainly will be dead. But we should arrange our earthly affairs, for the short run in which we have to live, in the best possible way. And one of the measures necessary for this purpose is to abandon inflationary policies.

Foreign Investment

Some people call the programs of economic freedom a negative program. They say: "What do you liberals really want? You are against socialism, government intervention, inflation, labor union violence, protective tariffs.... You say 'no' to everything."

I would call this statement a one-sided and shallow formulation of the problem. For it is possible to formulate a liberal program in a *positive* way. If a man says: "I am against censorship," he is not negative; he is *in favor* of authors having the right to determine what they want to publish without the interference of government. This is not negativism, this is precisely freedom. (Of course, when I use the term "liberal" with respect to the conditions of the economic system, I mean liberal in the old *classical* sense of the word.)

Today, most people regard the considerable differences in the standard of living between many countries as unsatisfactory. Two hundred years ago, conditions in Great Britain were much worse than they are today in India. But the British in 1750 did not call themselves "undeveloped" or "backward," because they were not in a position to compare the conditions of their country with those of countries in which economic conditions were more satisfactory. Today all people who have not attained the average standard of living of the United

States believe that there is something wrong with their own economic situation. Many of these countries call themselves "developing countries" and, as such, are asking for aid from the so-called developed or even overdeveloped countries.

Let me explain the reality of this situation. The standard of living is lower in the so-called developing countries because the average earnings for the same type of labor is lower in those countries than it is in some countries of Western Europe, Canada, Japan, and especially in the United States. If we try to find the reasons for this difference, we must realize that it is not due to an inferiority of the workers or other employees. There prevails among some groups of North American workers a tendency to believe that they themselves are better than other people—that it is through their own merit that they are getting higher wages than other people.

It would only be necessary for an American worker to visit another country—let us say, Italy, where many American workers came from—in order to discover that it is *not* his personal qualities but the conditions in the country that make it possible for him to earn higher wages. If a man from Sicily immigrates to the United States, he can very soon earn the wage rates that are customary in the United States. And if the same man returns to Sicily, he will discover that his visit to the United States did not give him qualities which would permit him to earn higher wages in Sicily than his fellow countrymen.

Nor can one explain this economic situation by assuming any inferiority on the part of entrepreneurs outside the United States. It is a fact that outside of the United States, Canada, Western Europe, and certain parts of Asia the equipment of the factories and the technological methods employed are, by and large, inferior to those within the United States. But this is not due to the ignorance of the entrepreneurs in those "undeveloped" countries. They know very well that the factories in the United States and Canada are much better equipped. They themselves know everything they must know about technology, and if they do not, they have the opportunity to learn what they must know from textbooks and technical magazines which disseminate this knowledge.

Once again: the difference is not personal inferiority or ignorance. The difference is the supply of capital, the quantity of capital goods available. In other words, the amount of capital invested per unit of the population is greater in the so-called advanced nations than in the developing nations.

A businessman cannot pay a worker more than the amount added by the work of his employee to the value of the product. He cannot pay him more than the customers are prepared to pay for the *additional* work of this individual worker. If he pays him more, he will not recover his expenditures from the customers. He incurs losses and, as I have pointed out again and again, and as everybody knows, a businessman who suffers losses must change his methods of business, or go bankrupt.

The economists describe this state of affairs by saying "wages are determined by the marginal productivity of labor." This is only another expression for what I have just said before. It is a fact that the scale of wages is determined by the amount a man's work increases the value of the product. If a man works with better and more efficient tools, then he can perform in one hour much more than a man who works one hour with less efficient instruments. It is obvious that 100 men working in an American shoe factory, equipped with the most modern tools and machines, produce much more in the same length of time than 100 shoemakers in India, who have to work with old-fashioned tools in a less sophisticated way.

The employers in all of these developing nations know very well that better tools would make their own enterprises more profitable. They would like to build more and better factories. The only thing that prevents them from doing it is the shortage of capital. The difference between the less developed and the more developed nations is a function of time: the British started to save sooner than all other nations: they also started to accumulate capital and to invest it in business. Because they started sooner, there was a higher standard of living in Great Britain when, in all other European countries, there was still a lower standard of living. Gradually, all the other nations began to study British conditions, and it was not difficult for them to discover the reason for Great Britain's wealth. So they began to imitate the methods of British business.

Since other nations started later, and since the British did not stop investing capital, there remained a large difference between conditions in England and conditions in those other countries. But something happened which caused the headstart of Great Britain to disappear.

What happened was the greatest event in the history of the nineteenth century, and this means not only in the history of an individual country. This great event was the development, in the nineteenth century, of *foreign investment*. In 1817, the great British economist Ricardo still took it for granted that capital could be invested only within the borders of a country. He took it for granted that capitalists would not try to invest abroad. But a few decades later, capital investment abroad began to play a most important role in world affairs.

Without capital investment, it would have been necessary for nations less developed than Great Britain to start with the methods and the technology with which the British had started, in the beginning and middle of the eighteenth century, and slowly, step by step—always far below the technological level of British economy—try to imitate what the British had done.

It would have taken many, many decades for these countries to attain the standard of technological development which Great Britain had reached a hundred years or more before them. But the great event that helped all these countries was foreign investment.

Foreign investment meant that British capitalists invested British capital in other parts of the world. They first invested it in those European countries which, from the point of view of Great Britain, were short of capital and backward in their development. It is a well-known fact that the railroads of most European countries, and also of the United States, were built with the aid of British capital. You know that the same happened in this country, in Argentina.

The gas companies in all the cities of Europe were also British. In the mid 1870s, a British author and poet criticized his countrymen. He said: "The British have lost their old vigour and they have no longer any new ideas. They are no longer an important or leading nation in the world." To which Herbert Spencer, the great sociologist, answered: "Look at the European continent. All European capitals have light because a British gas company provides them with gas." This was, of course, in what seems to us the "remote" age of gas lighting. Further answering this British critic, Herbert Spencer added:

"You say that the Germans are far ahead of Great Britain. But look at Germany. Even Berlin, the capital of the German Reich, the capital of *Geist*, would be in the dark if a British gas company had not invaded the country and lighted the streets."

In the same way, British capital developed the railroads and many branches of industry in the United States. And, of course, as long as a country imports capital, its balance of trade is what the noneconomists call "unfavorable." That means that it has an excess of imports over exports. The reason for the "favorable balance of trade" of Great Britain was that the British factories sent many types of equipment to the United States, and this equipment was not paid for by anything other than shares of American corporations. This period in the history of the United States lasted, by and large, until the 1890s.

But when the United States, with the aid of British capital—and later with the aid of its own procapitalistic policies—developed its own economic system in an unprecedented way, the Americans began to buy back the capital in stocks they had once sold to foreigners. Then the United States had a surplus of exports over imports. The difference was paid by the importation—by the repatriation, as one called it—of American common stock.

This period lasted until the First World War. What happened later is another story. It is the story of the American subsidies for the belligerent countries in, between, and after two world wars: the loans, the investments the United States made in Europe, in addition to lend-lease, foreign aid, the Marshall Plan, food that was sent overseas, and other subsidies. I emphasize this because people sometimes believe that it is shameful or degrading to have foreign capital working in their country. You have to realize that, in all countries except England, foreign capital investment played a considerable part in the development of modern industries.

If I say that foreign investment was the greatest historical event of the nineteenth century, you must think of all those things that would not have come into being if there had not been any foreign investment. All the railroads, the harbors, the factories and mines in Asia, and the Suez Canal and many other things in the Western hemisphere, would not have been constructed had there been no foreign investment.

Foreign investment is made in the expectation that it will not be expropriated. Nobody would invest anything if he knew in advance that somebody would expropriate his investments. At the time when these foreign investments were made in the nineteenth century, and at the beginning of the twentieth century, there was no question of expropriation. From the beginning, some countries showed a certain hostility toward foreign capital, but for the most part they realized very well that they derived an enormous advantage from these foreign investments.

In some cases, these foreign investments were not made directly to foreign capitalists, but indirectly by loans to the foreign government. Then it was the government that used the money for investments. Such was, for instance, the case in Russia. For purely political reasons, the French invested in Russia, in the two decades preceding the First World War, about twenty billion gold francs, lending them chiefly to the Russian government. All the great enterprises of the Russian government—for instance, the railroad that connects Russia from the Ural Mountains, through the ice and snow of Siberia, to the Pacific—were built mostly with foreign capital lent to the Russian government. You will realize that the French did not assume that, one day, there would be a communist Russian government that would simply declare it would not pay the debts incurred by its predecessor, the tsarist government.

Starting with the First World War, there began a period of worldwide open warfare against foreign investments. Since there is no remedy to prevent a government from expropriating invested capital, there is practically no legal protection for foreign investments in the world today. The capitalists did not forsee this. If the capitalists of the capital exporting countries had realized it, all foreign investments would have come to an end forty or fifty years ago. But the capitalists did not believe that any country would be so unethical as to renege on a debt, to expropriate and confiscate foreign capital. With these acts, a new chapter began in the economic history of the world.

With the end of the great period in the nineteenth century when foreign capital helped to develop, in all parts of the world, modern methods of transportation, manufacturing, mining, and agriculture, there came a new era in which the governments and the political parties considered the foreign investor as an *exploiter* who should be expelled from the country.

In this anti-capitalist attitude the Russians were not the only sinners. Remember, for example, the expropriation of the American oil fields in Mexico, and all the things that have happened in *this* country (Argentina) which I have no need to discuss.

The situation in the world today, created by the system of expropriation of foreign capital, consists either of direct expropriation or of indirect expropriation through foreign exchange control or tax discrimination. This is mainly a problem of developing nations.

Take, for instance, the biggest of these nations: India. Under the British system, British capital—predominately British capital, but also capital of other European countries—was invested in India. And the British exported to India something else which also has to be mentioned in this connection; they exported into India modern methods of fighting contagious diseases. The result was a tremendous increase in the Indian population and a corresponding increase in the country's troubles. Facing such a worsening situation, India turned to expropriation as a means of dealing with its problems. But it was not always direct expropriation; the government harassed foreign capitalists, hampering them in their investments in such a way that these foreign investors were forced to sell out.

India could, of course, accumulate capital by another method: the *domestic* accumulation of capital. However, India is as hostile to the domestic accumulation of capital as it is to foreign capitalists. The Indian government says it wants to industrialize India, but what it really has in mind is to have *socialist* enterprises.

A few years ago the famous statesman Jawaharlal Nehru published a collection of his speeches. The book was published with the intention of making foreign investment in India more attractive. The Indian government is not opposed to foreign investment *before* it is invested. The hostility begins only when it *is already* invested. In this book—I am quoting literally from the book—Mr. Nehru said: "Of course, we want to socialize. But we are not opposed to private enterprise. We want to encourage in every way private enterprise. We want to promise the entrepreneurs who invest in our country, that we will not expropriate them nor socialize them for ten years, perhaps even for a longer time." And he thought this was an invitation to come to India!

The problem—as you know—is domestic capital accumulation. In all countries today there are very heavy taxes on corporations. In fact, there is double taxation on corporations. First, the profits of corporations are taxed very heavily, and the dividends which corporations pay to their shareholders are taxed again. And this is done in a progressive way.

Progressive taxation of income and profits means that precisely those parts of the income which people would have saved and invested are taxed away. Take the example of the United States. A few years ago, there was an "excess-profit" tax, which meant that out of one dollar earned, a corporation retained only eighteen cents. When these eighteen cents were paid out to the shareholders, those who had a great number of shares had to pay another sixty or eighty or even greater percent of it in taxes. Out of the dollar of profit they retained about seven cents, and ninety-three cents went to the government. Of this ninety-three percent, the greater part would have been saved and invested. Instead, the government used it for current expenditure. This is the policy of the United States.

I think I have made it clear that the policy of the United States is not an example to be imitated by other countries. This policy of the United States is worse than bad—it is *insane*. The only thing I would add is that a rich country can afford more bad policies than a poor country. In the United States, in spite of all these methods of taxation, there is still some additional accumulation of capital and investment every year, and therefore there is still a trend toward an improvement of the standard of living.

But in many other countries the problem is very critical. There is no—or not sufficient—domestic saving, and capital investment from abroad is seriously reduced by the fact that these countries are openly hostile to foreign investment. How can they talk about industrialization, about the necessity to develop new plants, to improve conditions, to raise the standard of living, to have higher wage rates, better means of transportation, if these countries are doing things that will have precisely the opposite effect? What their policies actually accomplish is to prevent or to slow down the accumulation of domestic capital and to put obstacles in the way of foreign capital.

The end result is certainly very bad. Such a situation must bring about a loss of confidence, and there is now more and more distrust of foreign investment in the world. Even if the countries concerned were to change their policies immediately and were to make all possible promises, it is very doubtful that they could once more inspire foreign capitalists to invest.

There are, of course, some methods to avoid this consequence. One could establish some international statutes, not only agreements, that would withdraw the foreign investments from national jurisdiction. This is something the United Nations could do. But the United Nations is simply a meeting place for useless discussions. Realizing the enormous importance of foreign investment, realizing that foreign investment alone can bring about an improvement in political and economical world conditions, one could try to do something from the point of view of international legislation.

This is a technical legal problem, which I only mention, because the situation is not hopeless. If the world really

wanted to make it possible for the developing countries
to raise their standard of living to the level of the American way of life, then it could be done. It is only necessary
to realize *how* it could be done.

What is lacking in order to make the developing countries as prosperous as the United States is only one thing:
capital—and, of course, the freedom to employ it under
the discipline of the market and not the discipline of the
government. These nations must accumulate domestic
capital, and they must make it possible for foreign capital
to come into their countries.

For the development of domestic saving it is necessary
to mention again that domestic saving by the masses of
the population presupposes a stable monetary unit. This
implies the absence of *any* kind of inflation.

A great part of the capital at work in American enterprises is owned by the workers themselves and by other
people with modest means. Billions and billions of saving deposits, of bonds, and of insurance policies are
operating in these enterprises. On the American money
market today it is no longer the banks, it is the insurance
companies that are the greatest money lenders. And the
money of the insurance company is—not legally, but
economically—the property of the insured. And practically everybody in the United States is insured in one
way or another.

The prerequisite for more economic equality in the
world is industrialization. And this is possible only
through increased capital investment, increased capital
accumulation. You may be astonished that I have not
mentioned a measure which is considered a prime
method to industrialize a country. I mean...protec-
tionism. But tariffs and foreign exchange controls are
exactly the means to *prevent* the importation of capital

and industrialization into the country. The only way to increase industrialization is to have more capital. Protectionism can only divert investments from one branch of business to another branch.

Protectionism, in itself, does not add anything to the capital of a country. To start a new factory one needs capital. To improve an already existing factory one needs capital, and not a tariff.

I do not want to discuss the whole problem of free trade or protectionism. I hope that most of your textbooks on economics represent it in a proper way. Protection does not change the economic situation in a country for the better. And what *certainly* does not change it for the better is labor unionism. If conditions are unsatisfactory, if wages are low, if the wage earner in a country looks to the United States and reads about what is going on there, if he sees in the movies how the home of an average American is equipped with all modern comforts, he may be envious. He is perfectly right in saying: "We ought to have the same thing." But the only way to obtain it is through an increase in capital.

Labor unions use violence against entrepreneurs and against people they call strikebreakers. Despite their power and their violence, however, unions cannot raise wages continually for all wage earners. Equally ineffective are government decrees fixing minimum wage rates. What the unions *do* bring about (if they succeed in raising wage rates) is permanent, lasting unemployment.

But unions cannot industrialize the country, they cannot raise the standard of living of the workers. And this is the decisive point: One must realize that all the policies of a country that wants to improve its standard of living must be directed toward an increase in the capital invested per capita. This per capita investment of capital is

still increasing in the United States, in spite of all of the
bad policies there. And the same is true in Canada and in
some of the West European countries. But it is unfortunately decreasing in countries like India.

We read every day in the newspapers that the population of the world is becoming greater, by perhaps 45
million people—or even more—per year. And how will
this end? What will the results and the consequences be?
Remember what I said about Great Britain. In 1750 the
British people believed that six million constituted a tremendous overpopulation of the British Isles and that
they were headed for famines and plagues. But on the
eve of the last world war, in 1939, fifty million people
were living in the British Isles, and the standard of living
was incomparably higher than it had been in 1750. This
was the effect of what is called industrialization—a rather
inadequate term.

Britain's progress was brought about by increasing the
per capita investment of capital. As I said before. . . there
is only one way a nation can achieve prosperity: if you
increase capital, you increase the marginal productivity
of labor, and the effect will be that real wages will rise.

In a world without migration barriers, there would be a
tendency all over the world toward an equalization of
wage rates. If there were no migration barriers today,
probably twenty million people would try to reach the
United States every year, in order to get higher wages.
The inflow would reduce wages in the United States, and
raise them in other countries.

I do not have time to deal with this problem of migration barriers. But I do want to say that there is another
method toward the equalization of wage rates all over the
world. This other method, which operates in the absence
of the freedom to migrate, is the *migration of capital*.

Capitalists have the tendency to move towards those countries in which there is plenty of labor available and in which labor is reasonable. And by the fact that they bring capital into these countries, they bring about a trend toward higher wage rates. This has worked in the past, and it will work in the future, in the same way.

When British capital was first invested in, let us say, Austria or Bolivia, wage rates there were much, much lower than they were in Great Britain. But this additional investment brought about a trend toward higher wage rates in those countries. And such a tendency prevailed all over the world. It is a very well-known fact that as soon as, for instance, the United Fruit Company moved into Guatemala, the result was a general tendency toward higher wage rates, beginning with the wages which United Fruit Company paid, which then made it necessary for other employers to pay higher wages also. Therefore, there is no reason at all to be pessimistic in regard to the future of "undeveloped" countries.

I fully agree with the Communists and the labor unions, when they say: "What is needed is to raise the standard of living." A short time ago, in a book published in the United States, a professor said: "We now have enough of everything, why should people in the world still work so hard? We have everything already." I do not doubt that this professor has everything. But there are other people in other countries, also many people in the United States, who want and should have a better standard of living.

Outside of the United States—in Latin America, and still more in Asia and Africa—everyone wishes to see conditions improved in his own country. A higher standard of living also brings about a higher standard of culture and civilization.

So I fully agree with the ultimate goal of raising the standard of living everywhere. But I disagree about the measures to be adopted in attaining this goal. What measures will attain this end? Not protection, not government interference, not socialism, and certainly not the violence of the labor unions (euphemistically called collective bargaining, which, in fact, is bargaining *at the point of a gun*).

To attain the end, as I see it, there is only one way! It is a slow method. Some people may say, it is too slow. But there are no short cuts to an earthly paradise. It takes time, and one has to work. But it does not take as much time as people believe, and finally an equalization will come.

Around 1840, in the western part of Germany—in Swabia and Württemberg, which was one of the most industrialized areas in the world—it was said: "We can never attain the level of the British. The English have a head start, and they will forever be ahead of us." Thirty years later the British said: "This German competition, we cannot stand it, we have to do something against it." At that time, of course, the German standard was rapidly rising and was, even then, approaching the British standard. And today the German income per capita is not behind that of Great Britain at all.

In the center of Europe, there is a small country, Switzerland, which nature has endowed very poorly. It has no coal mines, no minerals, and no natural resources. But its people, over the centuries, have continually pursued a capitalistic policy. They have developed the highest standard of living in continental Europe, and their country ranks as one of the world's great centers of civilization. I do not see why a country such as Argentina—which is much larger than Switzerland both

in population and in size—should not attain the same
high standard of living after some years of good policies.
But—as I pointed out—the policies must be good.

Politics and Ideas

In the Age of Enlightenment, in the years in which the North Americans founded their independence, and a few years later, when the Spanish and Portuguese colonies were transformed into independent nations, the prevailing mood in Western civilization was optimistic. At that time all philosophers and statesmen were fully convinced that we were living at the beginning of a new age of prosperity, progress, and freedom. In those days people expected that the new political institutions—the constitutional representative governments established in the free nations of Europe and America—would work in a very beneficial way, and that economic freedom would continuously improve the material conditions of mankind.

We know very well that some of these expectations were too optimistic. It is certainly true that we have experienced, in the nineteenth and twentieth centuries, an unprecented improvement in economic conditions, making it possible for a much larger population to live at a much higher standard of living. But we also know that many of the hopes of the eighteenth century philosophers have been badly shattered—hopes that there would not be any more wars and that revolutions would become unnecessary. These expectations were not realized.

During the nineteenth century, there was a period when wars decreased in both number and severity. But the twentieth century brought a resurgence of the war-like spirit, and we can fairly well say that we may not yet be at the end of the trials through which mankind will have to go.

The constitutional system that began at the end of the eighteenth and the beginning of the nineteenth century has disappointed mankind. Most people—also most authors—who have dealt with this problem seem to think there has been no connection between the economic and the political side of the problem. Thus, they tend to deal at great length with the decay of parliamentarism—government by the representatives of the people—as if this phenomenon were completely independent of the economic situation and of the economic ideas that determine the activities of people.

But such an independence does not exist. Man is not a being that, on the one hand, has an economic side and, on the other hand, a political side, with no connection between the two. In fact, what is called the decay of freedom, of constitutional government and representative institutions, is the consequence of the radical change in economic and political ideas. The political events are the inevitable consequence of the change in economic policies.

The ideas that guided the statesmen, philosophers and lawyers who, in the eighteenth century and in the early nineteenth century developed the fundamentals of the new political system, started from the assumption that, within a nation, all honest citizens have the same ultimate goal. This ultimate goal, to which all decent men should be dedicated, is the welfare of the whole nation, and also the welfare of other nations—these moral and political leaders being fully convinced that a free nation is not interested in conquest. They conceived of party strife as only natural, that it was perfectly normal for there to be differences of opinion concerning the best way to conduct the affairs of state.

Those people who held similar ideas about a problem cooperated, and this cooperation was called a party. But a party structure was not permanent. It did not depend on the position of the individuals within the whole social structure. It could change if people learned that their original position was based on erroneous assumptions, on erroneous ideas. From this point of view, many regarded the discussions in the election campaigns and later in the legislative assemblies as an important political factor. The speeches of members of a legislature were not considered to be merely pronouncements telling the world what a political party wanted. They were regarded as attempts to convince opposing groups that the speaker's own ideas were more correct, more beneficial to the common weal, than those which they had heard before.

Political speeches, editorials in newspapers, pamphlets, and books were written in order to persuade. There was little reason to believe that one could not convince the majority that one's own position was absolutely correct if one's ideas were sound. It was from this point of view that the constitutional rules were written in the legislative bodies of the early nineteenth century.

But this implied that the government would not interfere with the economic conditions of the market. It implied that all citizens had only one political aim: the welfare of the whole country and of the whole nation. And it is precisely this social and economic philosophy that interventionism has replaced. Interventionism has spawned a very different philosophy.

Under interventionist ideas, it is the duty of the government to support, to subsidize, to give privileges to special groups. The idea of the eighteenth century statesmen was that the legislators had special ideas about the common good. But what we have today, what we see today in the reality of political life, practically without any exceptions, in all the countries of the world where there is not simply communist dictatorship, is a situation where there are no longer real political parties in the old classical sense, but merely *pressure groups*.

A pressure group is a group of people who want to attain for themselves a special privilege at the expense of the rest of the nation. This privilege may consist in a tariff on competing imports, it may consist in a subsidy, it may consist in laws that prevent other people from competing with the members of the pressure group. At any rate, it gives to the members of the pressure group a special position. It gives them something which is denied or ought to be denied—according to the ideas of the pressure group—to other groups.

In the United States, the two-party system of the old days is seemingly still preserved. But this is only a camouflage of the real situation. In fact, the political life of the United States—as well as the political life of all other countries—is determined by the struggle and aspirations of pressure groups. In the United States there is still a Republican party and a Democratic party, but in each of these parties there are pressure group representatives. These pressure group representatives are more interested in cooperation with representatives of the same pressure group in the opposing party than with the efforts of fellow members in their own party.

To give you an example, if you talk to people in the United States who really know the business of Congress, they will tell you: "This man, this member of Congress represents the interests of the silver groups." Or they will tell you another man represents the wheat growers.

Of course, each of these pressure groups is necessarily a minority. In a system based on the division of labor, every special group that aims at privileges has to be a minority. And minorities never have the chance to attain success, if they do not cooperate with other similar minorities, similar pressure groups. In the legislative assemblies, they try to bring about a coalition between various pressure groups, so that they might become the majority. But, after a time, this coalition may disintegrate, because there are problems on which it is impossible to reach agreement with other pressure groups, and new pressure group coalitions are formed.

That is what happened in France in 1871, a situation which historians deemed "the decay of the Third Republic." It was not a decay of the Third Republic; it was simply an exemplification of the fact that the pressure group system is not a system that can be successfully applied to the government of a big nation.

You have, in the legislatures, representatives of wheat, of meat, of silver, and of oil, but first of all, of the various unions. Only one thing is *not* represented in the legislature: the nation as a whole. There are only a few who take the side of the nation as a whole. And all problems, even those of foreign policy, are seen from the point of view of the special pressure group interests.

In the United States, some of the less-populated states are interested in the price of silver. But not everybody in these states is interested in it. Nevertheless, the United States, for many decades, has spent a considerable sum of money, at the expense of the taxpayers, in order to buy silver above its market price. For another example, in the United States only a small proportion of the population is employed in agriculture; the remainder of the population is made up of consumers—but not producers—of agricultural products. The United States, nevertheless, has a policy of spending billions and billions in order to keep the prices of agricultural products above the potential market price.

One cannot say that this is a policy in favor of a small minority, because these agricultural interests are not uniform. The dairy farmer is not interested in a high price for cereals; on the contrary, he would prefer a lower price for this product. A chicken farmer wants a lower price for chicken feed. There are many incompatible special interests within this group. And yet, clever diplomacy in congressional politics makes it possible for small minority groups to get privileges at the expense of the majority.

One situation, especially interesting in the United States, concerns sugar. Perhaps only one out of 500 Americans is interested in a higher price for sugar. Probably 499 out of 500 want a lower price for sugar. Nevertheless, the policy of the United States is committed, by tariffs and other special measures, to a higher price for sugar. This policy is not only detrimental to the interests of those 499 who are consumers of sugar, it also creates a very severe problem of foreign policy for the United States. The aim of foreign policy is cooperation with all other American republics, some of which are interested in selling sugar to the United States. They would like to sell a greater quantity of it. This illustrates how pressure group interests may determine even the foreign policy of a nation.

For years, people throughout the world have been

writing about democracy—about popular, representative government. They have been complaining about its inadequacies, but the democracy they criticize is only that democracy under which *interventionism* is the governing policy of the country.

Today one might hear people say: "In the early nineteenth century, in the legislatures of France, England, the United States, and other nations, there were speeches about the great problems of mankind. They fought against tyranny, for freedom, for cooperation with all other free nations. But now we are more practical in the legislature!"

Of course we are more practical; people today do not talk about freedom: they talk about a *higher price for peanuts*. If this is practical, then of course the legislatures have changed considerably, but not improved.

These political changes, brought about by interventionism, have considerably weakened the power of nations and of representatives to resist the aspirations of dictators and the operations of tyrants. The legislative representatives whose only concern is to satisfy the voters who want, for instance, a high price for sugar, milk, and butter, and a low price for wheat (subsidized by the government) can represent the people only in a very weak way; they can never represent *all* their constituents.

The voters who are in favor of such privileges do not realize that there are also opponents who want the opposite thing and who prevent *their* representatives from achieving full success.

This system leads also to a constant increase of public expenditures, on the one hand, and makes it more difficult, on the other, to levy taxes. These pressure group representatives want many special privileges for their pressure groups, but they do not want to burden their supporters with a too-heavy tax load.

It was not the idea of the eighteenth century founders of modern constitutional government that a legislator should represent *not* the whole nation but only the special interests of the district in which he was elected; that was one of the consequences of interventionism. The original idea was that every member of the legislature *should* represent the whole nation. He was elected in a special district only because there he was known and elected by people who had confidence in him.

But it was not intended that he go into government in order to procure something special for his constituency, that he ask for a new school or a new hospital or a new lunatic asylum—thereby causing a considerable rise in government expenditures within his district. Pressure group politics explains why it is almost impossible, for all governments, to stop inflation. As soon as the elected officials try to restrict expenditures, to limit spending, those who support special interests, who derive advantages from special items in the budget, come and declare that *this* particular project cannot be undertaken, or that *that one* must be done.

Dictatorship, of course, is no solution to the problems of economics, just as it is not the answer to the problems of freedom. A dictator may start out by making promises of every sort but, being a dictator, he will not keep his promises. He will, instead, suppress free speech immediately, so that the newspapers and the legislative speech-makers will not be able to point out—days, months or years afterwards—that he said something different on the first day of his dictatorship than he did later on.

The terrible dictatorship which such a big country as

Germany had to live through in the recent past comes to mind, as we look upon the decline of freedom in so many countries today. As a result, people speak now about the decay of freedom and about the decline of our civilization.

People say that every civilization must finally fall into ruin and disintegrate. There are eminent supporters of this idea. One was a German teacher, Spengler, and another one, much better known, was the English historian Toynbee. They tell us that our civilization is now old. Spengler compared civilization to plants which grow and grow, but whose life finally comes to an end. The same, he says, is true for civilizations. The metaphorical likening of a civilization to a plant is completely arbitrary.

First of all, it is within the history of mankind very difficult to distinguish between different, independent civilizations. Civilizations are not independent; they are *interdependent*, they constantly influence each other. One cannot speak of the decline of a particular civilization, therefore, in the same way that one can speak of the death of a particular plant.

But even if you refute the doctrines of Spengler and Toynbee, a very popular comparison still remains: the comparison of decaying civilizations. It is certainly true that in the second century A.D., the Roman Empire nurtured a very flourishing civilization, that in those parts of Europe, Asia, and Africa in which the Roman Empire ruled, there was a very high civilization. There was also a very high *economic* civilization, based on a certain degree of division of labor. Although it appears quite primitive when compared with our conditions today, it certainly was remarkable. It reached the highest degree of the division of labor ever attained before modern capitalism. It is no less true that this civilization disintegrated, especially in the third century. This disintegration within the Roman Empire made it impossible for the Romans to resist aggression from without. Although the aggression was no worse than that which the Romans had resisted again and again in the preceding centuries, they could withstand it no longer after what had taken place within the Roman Empire.

What had taken place? What was the problem? What was it that caused the disintegration of an empire which, in every regard, had attained the highest civilization ever achieved before the eighteenth century? The truth is that what destroyed this ancient civilization was something similar, almost identical to the dangers that threaten our civilization today: on the one hand it was *interventionism*, and on the other hand, *inflation*. The interventionism of the Roman Empire consisted in the fact that the Roman Empire, following the preceding Greek policy, did not abstain from price control. This price control was mild, practically without any consequences, because for centuries it did not try to reduce prices below the market level.

But when inflation began in the third century, the poor Romans did not yet have our technical means for inflation—they could not print money. They had to debase the coinage, and this was a much inferior system of inflation compared to the present system, which—through the use of the modern printing press—can so easily destroy the value of money. But it was efficient enough, and it brought about the same result as price control. For the prices which the authorities tolerated were now below the potential price to which inflation had brought the prices of the various commodities.

The result, of course, was that the supply of foodstuffs in the cities declined. The people in the cities were forced to go back to the country and to return to agricultural life. The Romans never realized what was happening. They did not understand it. They had not developed the mental tools to interpret the problems of the division of labor and the consequences of inflation upon market prices. That this currency inflation, currency debasement, was bad, this they knew of course very well.

Consequently, the emperors made laws against this movement. There were laws preventing the city dweller from moving to the country, but such laws were ineffective. As the people did not have anything to eat in the city, as they were starving, no law could keep them from leaving the city and going back into agriculture. The city dweller could no longer work in the processing industries of the cities as an artisan. And, with the loss of the markets in the cities, no one could buy anything there anymore.

Thus we see that, from the third century on, the cities of the Roman Empire were declining and that the division of labor became less intensive than it had been before. Finally, the medieval system of the self-sufficient household, of the "villa," as it was called in later laws, emerged.

Therefore, if people compare our conditions with those of the Roman Empire and say: "We will go the same way," they have some reasons for saying so. They can find some facts which are similar. But there are also enormous differences. These differences are not in the political structure which prevailed in the second part of the third century. Then, on the average of every three years, an emperor was assassinated, and the man who killed him or had caused his death became his successor. After three years, on the average, the same happened to the new emperor. When Diocletian, in the year 284, became emperor, he tried for some time to oppose the decay, but without success.

There are enormous differences between present-day conditions and those that prevailed in Rome, in that the measures that caused the disintegration of the Roman Empire were not premeditated. They were not, I would say, the result of reprehensible formalized doctrines.

In contrast, however, the interventionist ideas, the socialist ideas, the inflationist ideas of our time, have been concocted and formalized by writers and professors. And they are taught at colleges and universities. You may say: "Today's situation is much worse." I will answer: "No, it is not worse." It is better, in my opinion, because ideas can be defeated by other ideas. Nobody doubted, in the age of the Roman emperors, that the government had the right and that it was a good policy to determine maximum prices. Nobody disputed this.

But now that we have schools and professors and books that recommend this, we know very well that this is a problem for discussion. All these bad ideas from which we suffer today, which have made our policies so harmful, were developed by academic theorists.

A famous Spanish author spoke about "the revolt of the masses." We have to be very cautious in using this term, because this revolt was not made by the masses: it was made by the intellectuals. And those intellectuals who developed these doctrines were not men from the masses. The Marxian doctrine pretends that it is only the proletarians that have the good ideas and that only the proletarian mind created socialism. All the socialist authors, without exception, were *bourgeois* in the sense in which the socialists use this term.

Karl Marx was *not* a man from the proletariat. He was the son of a lawyer. He did not have to work to go to the university. He studied at the university in the same way as do the sons of well-to-do people today. Later, and for the rest of his life, he was supported by his friend Friedrich Engels, who—being a manufacturer—was the worst type of "bourgeois," according to socialist ideas. In the language of Marxism, he was an exploiter.

Everything that happens in the social world in our time is the result of ideas. Good things and bad things. What is needed is to fight bad ideas. We must fight all that we dislike in public life. We must substitute better ideas for wrong ideas. We must refute the doctrines that promote union violence. We must oppose the confiscation of property, the control of prices, inflation, and all those evils from which we suffer.

Ideas and only ideas can light the darkness. These ideas must be brought to the public in such a way that they persuade people. We must convince them that these ideas are the right ideas and not the wrong ones. The great age of the nineteenth century, the great achievements of capitalism, were the result of the ideas of the classical economists, of Adam Smith and David Ricardo, of Bastiat and others.

What we need is nothing else than to substitute better ideas for bad ideas. This, I hope and am confident, will be done by the rising generation. Our civilization is not doomed, as Spengler and Toynbee tell us. Our civilization will not be conquered by the spirit of Moscow. Our civilization will and must survive. And it will survive through better ideas than those which now govern most of the world today, and these better ideas will be developed by the rising generation.

I consider it as a very good sign that, while fifty years ago, practically nobody in the world had the courage to say anything in favor of a free economy, we have now, at least in some of the advanced countries of the world, institutions that are centers for the propagation of a free economy, such as, for example, the "Centre" in your country which invited me to come to Buenos Aires, to say a few words in this great city.

I could not say much about these important matters. Six lectures may be very much for an audience, but they are not enough to develop the whole philosophy of a free economic system, and certainly not enough to refute all the nonsense that has been written in the last fifty years about the economic problems with which we are dealing.

I am very grateful to this center for giving me the opportunity to address such a distinguished audience, and I hope that in a few years the number of those who are supporting ideas for freedom in this country, and in other countries, will increase considerably. I myself have full confidence in the future of freedom, both political and economic.